gardening in
TORONTO

gardening in TORONTO

by
PAT TUCKER

Technical Editor
BRIAN ANDREWS

LONE PINE

The Publisher:
Lone Pine Publishing
206, 10426-81 Avenue
Edmonton, Alberta, Canada
T6E 1X5

Canadian Cataloguing in Publication Data
Tucker, P. J.
Gardening in Toronto

Includes bibliographical references and index.
ISBN 0-919433-68-5
1. Gardening--Ontario--Toronto.   I. Title.
SB453.3.C2T83 1991   635'.09713'54   C91-091283-1

Technical editor: *Brian Andrews*
Editors: *Phillip Kennedy, Gary Whyte, Jane Spalding*
Designer: *Beata Kurpinski*
Printer: *Jasper Printing Group Ltd., Edmonton, Alberta, Canada*

Cover photo: *Don Hamilton*
Front cover inset photo: *Adrian Thysse*
Back cover inset photo: *Brian Andrews*

The publisher gratefully acknowledges the assistance of the Federal Department of Communications, Alberta Culture and Multiculturalism, the Canada Council and the Alberta Foundation for the Literary Arts in the publication of this book.

All interior photographs by *Brian Andrews* except the following:
Pat Tucker: p.56 (top); p.57 (bottom); p.114 (bottom); p.117 (bottom); p.122 (bottom); p.123 (both); p.124 (bottom)
Don Hamilton: p.49-52

CONTENTS

ACKNOWLEDGEMENTS

With such a comprehensive endeavour, one has to turn to many sources of information. I would like to recognize the authors of the Ontario Ministry of Agriculture and Food bulletins on large and small fruit culture, and perennial lists from *Canadian Garden Perennials* by Art Buckley. Thanks to the staff of the Civic Garden Centre, Toronto, for supplying sources of photogenic gardens, and to those owners Dennis Campeau, Murray Haigh and Dr. Henry Landis, Q.C. who allowed their gardens to be used as subjects, and to Mr. Don Hamilton, photographer, for his time and technique. Finally a thanks to my wife and partner, Ruth, who transcribed the manuscript, often from tape, and kept the prose in line.

Pat Tucker

Are you intrigued by stories of the old Victory Gardens, but are unfamiliar with gardening? Have you always wanted to add a bit of colour to your barren balcony or city block? Or do you enjoy the taste of clean, fresh vegetables in the summer, but are inexperienced in raising plants? *Gardening in Toronto* will answer your questions concerning basic methods and techniques, and will serve as a guide to planning and designing everything from ornamental lawns to window-box arrangements.

Gardening in Toronto will also shatter a few myths. Some books on gardening give the impression that the beginner must already be familiar with arcane processes and long tables of statistics, even before planting the first seeds. Others imply that only expansive gardens on large lots are worthwhile, whereas in truth, anyone with even a small space can produce beautiful results.

Gardening in Toronto is the first of a cross-Canada series of local gardening manuals. The beginner will find much common sense here, while the more experienced gardener may pick up some new ideas. All will benefit from the local emphasis of the book. Far too many gardening books are steeped in generalizations about "generally hardy" plants or plants "suitable for most northern locales." Every variety of flower, tree, shrub, vegetable and grass in this book is specifically suited for the Toronto metropolitan region. What is presented here is definitely applicable to your climate. Additional books will soon appear for Halifax, Vancouver, Calgary and other major Canadian centres.

Gardening in Toronto is arranged in coherent, free-standing sections. The beginner can start by reading the first three chapters, on the area's geographic location and climate, basic garden planning, and the improvement of soil; the beginner might also take a quick look at *Chapter Ten*, as it contains valuable information on controlling pests and diseases. Those with limited space will find *Chapter Four: Gardening in Small Spaces* most helpful. The remaining chapters deal with specific aspects of gardening, including fruits, vegetables, trees and shrubs, flowers and lawns, which can be read as required.

Gardening in Toronto is for the modern city dweller. Those concerned with the environment will find helpful advice for introducing "green" into a variety of urban settings. Gardeners will also find topics treated with consideration and common sense. This is not an inflexible, judgmental textbook; it recognizes the fact that readers are rational adults who can make decisions for themselves.

Beginners may have the impression that gardening consists of endless hours of backbreaking, unrewarding toil under the hot sun. This does not need to be true; gardening can be both rewarding and fun. A well-kept lawn, the first red apple of the season, a basket of tangy tomatoes and crisp orange carrots, even the pot of begonias on the patio all produce the same effect: satisfaction in growing something of your own and in a job well done. Use this book as a guide. Experiment with the possible combinations. Most of all, enjoy yourself.

CHAPTER 1
GEOGRAPHY & CLIMATE

Canada's largest city, Metropolitan Toronto (population 3,141,000), is located on the northern shores of Lake Ontario at 43°39'N latitude and 79°23'W longitude, at an elevation of 122 m above sea level. Rolling topography rising to the north is intersected by major rivers — the Credit to the west and the Humber, Don and Rouge to the east. Their upper watersheds are either in a natural state or are recreational lands. Lower reaches are heavily urbanized.

Soils range from slightly acidic at Port Credit to alkaline in north and east Metro. They vary from well drained sandy loams to poorly drained heavy clays. Nevertheless, fruit and general farming were viable operations prior to urban expansion.

The natural vegetation is dominated by the eastern deciduous forest, remnants of which occur on the steep river ravine banks and bottom lands. Common native trees include sugar maple, beech, basswood, red ash, white oak and butternut. Black walnut, sycamore and red and silver maples are found in river valleys. Conifers are relatively scarce, although there are scattered stands of eastern white pine, tamarack and eastern hemlock.

Understorey plants include alternate-leaf dogwood, downy serviceberry and wild plum. In spring the forest floor is carpeted with white trillium and scattered groups of red trillium and hepatica.

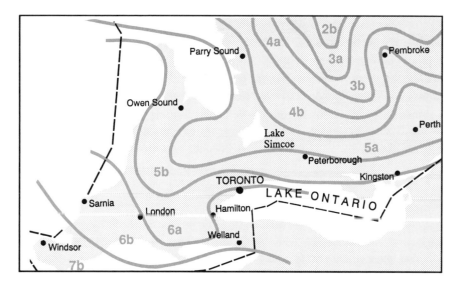

CLIMATE

Influenced by the waters of Lake Ontario, winters are relatively mild, and summers hot and humid. The annual mean temperature is 8.7°C. Winter lows range from -15°C downtown to -20°C in the suburbs, with highs of 10°C. The average winter low is -7°C.

Summer highs can reach 35°C, and average frost-free periods vary from 191 days downtown to 164 days in the suburbs. The effective growing season in an average year starts April 12th and finishes by November 9th. Average annual precipitation, primarily in the form of rain, is 776 mm, most of which occurs between October and mid-May.

Prevailing winds are primarily from the northwest, with warm southerlies during the summer and occasional cool easterlies in both summer and winter.

SEASONS

Spring can begin as early as April 1st, but frost may not be out of the soil before mid-April. Temperatures can escalate to 28°C by the third week in April, resulting in a short spring. On average, the last frost occurs on May 5, downtown, and May 10 in the suburbs.

Warm to hot and humid summers can be stressful to new plantings, particularly when rains are infrequent, and supplementary irrigation is often required. Cool nights and bright, balmy (19°C) fall days produce the glorious red, orange and yellow autumn colours of the eastern deciduous forest, providing an extended season for the gardener. Permanent frost does not occur until early December.

Winters vary from mild, as we experienced during the 1980s, to the very cold temperatures which typified the winters of the 1970s. Snow generally falls from late December to early March.

EFFECTS OF CLIMATE

Hardiness may be defined as the ability of a tree or shrub to withstand minimal winter temperatures and exposure, with little or no damage to its vegetative shoots and flower buds.

Canadian plant hardiness zones have been categorized, based on several climatic factors. The major factor is minimum temperature during winter. Other considerations are the frost-free period, summer rainfall, maximum summer temperatures, snow cover and wind.

The Canada Department of Agriculture has developed a map for the horticultural industry and gardeners, comprising ten zones, from which a tree or shrub's hardiness and locational preferences can be determined. Zone 0 is above the tree line in the tundra, where no trees grow, while Zone 9 incorporates the mildest areas of Canada, such as Victoria, B.C., and the Gulf Islands. Each zone is further divided into a colder part (a) and a warmer part (b).

Toronto is in Zone 6, with areas to the north of Highway 401 falling in 6a, and those closest to the lake in Zone 6b. The division between Zones 6a and 6b is arbitrary, as areas with their own microclimates may occur anywhere. In Zone 6a, for example, such influences as high land to the northwest, the proximity of bush areas, tall buildings and large bodies of water, may produce conditions which allow such trees as the Japanese maple, which does not normally survive in Zone 6a, to grow.

Orientation of one's own house can result in microclimates for tender plants. My back yard, for instance, is protected by the house and set in a bank to the north. This stimulates daffodils to bloom at least two weeks earlier in the back than at the front of the house, which is subject to northwest winds funnelling up the street.

TREES AND SHRUBS

Winter injury can occur in many forms, varying from minor twig damage to death. Poor bud break, resulting in dead or aborted flower buds, may occur in trees and shrubs that are marginally hardy. Flower buds are particularly susceptible since they are often less hardy than vegetative or leaf and shoot buds. Forsythia and saucer magnolia are vulnerable to low winter temperatures. The record low temperatures of -33.5°C which occurred in the winter of 1980-81 resulted in vegetative bud and stem injury on privet and Skogholm cotoneaster.

Crotch bark injury may occur in trees with narrow branch angles, since these areas do not harden off well in fall. Honey-locust is subject to this problem. Tree bark exposed to the southwest can suffer injury on bright sunny, winter days due to warm bark expanding, then contracting when temperatures drop. This freeze-thaw action causes a split in the trunk, often called south-west injury. Bright sunshine reflected by snow onto evergreen foliage can cause dessication and browning of needles, or sunscald.

Branch tip die-back is also common, particularly if branches do not harden off in late fall.

CLIMATE CONTROL

Creating wind breaks and planting close to the shelter of the house or boundary fences will minimize winter injury. Tree-wraps (wrapping tree trunks with burlap strips or special plastic spiral protectors) will control south-west injury. Correct pruning to eliminate narrow branch angles can minimize crotch injury. Plant selection for location and hardiness is the most critical factor when dealing with winter problems.

Although the climate in and around the garden may have adverse effects on plant growth, good garden practices such as correct planting procedures, pruning, fertilizing, irrigation and provision of good drainage will minimize the effects of climatic problems.

CHAPTER 2

GARDEN PLANNING

Planning is a creative activity. It involves anticipating future events and making decisions to accommodate them.

In any major gardening project, planning should always precede action. Planning involves deciding:

- What activities are wanted in the garden
- What features the garden will contain
- How much space will be required for each activity and feature
- Where the spaces for each activity and feature will be placed, and in what relationship to one another
- How function and form may be integrated to result in a comfortable, easily used and beautiful garden

Answers to these and related questions will form the basis of a blueprint for the development of a garden.Well conceived and well drawn plans reduce errors. They save time, energy and money.

The planning process begins with taking stock. This involves collecting and preparing certain kinds of information.

A DESIGN PROGRAM

Develop a well-articulated but simple written statement of design objectives. In other words, make a list of all the needs and wants that you intend your garden to satisfy. Outline how they can be accommodated in relation to site characteristics and limitations, and develop solutions to anticipated problems.

SITE PLAN

Prepare a plan, accurately drawn to scale, showing the exact location of all established features on the land surface, as well as those that run underground or above the site. Use various styles of broken and dotted lines to symbolize sewer, power, water, property lines and so on. A few contour lines to indicate slopes, hills, hollows and other major changes in elevations should be included where appropriate. Also indicate where shade will be cast during all seasons by the house, garage and any permanent trees.

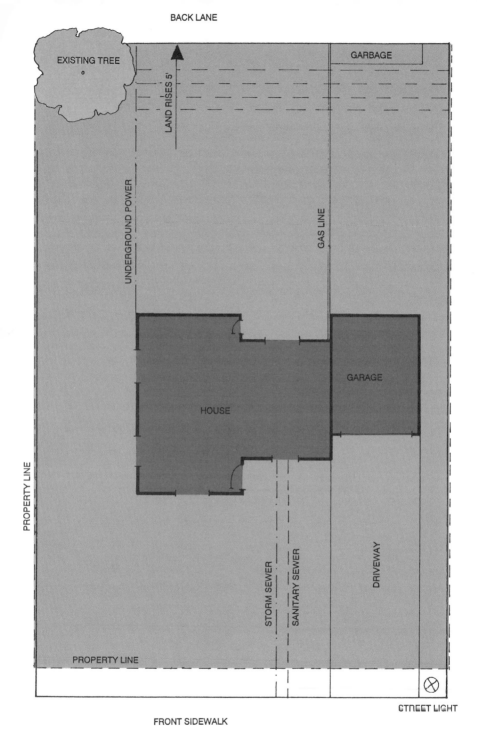

The Site Plan

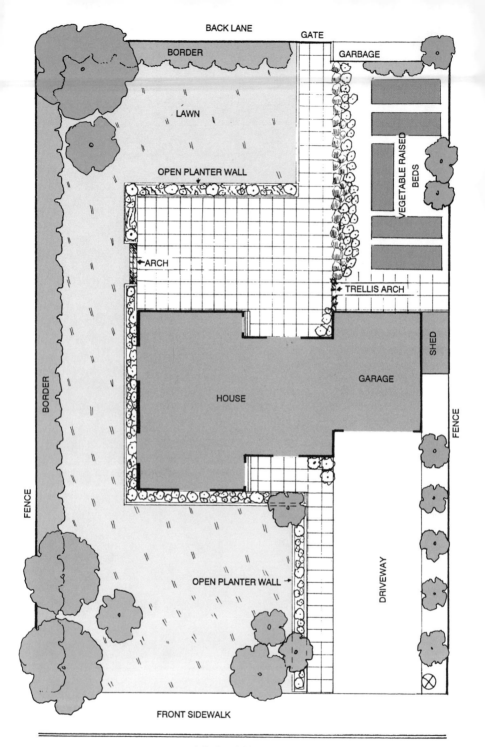

A Refined Sketch Plan

OFF SITE FEATURES

Make an inventory of features that are not on your site but may affect your plans. Include pleasant and unpleasant views, trees and vistas that you want to frame, in order to visually incorporate them into your landscape. Also include features that need to be screened. Include these items on your site plan, outside the property lines, in the form of notes and arrows.

THE HOUSE

On the site plan, locate the house and note the size, shape and elevations of all rooms, windows, doors, decks, steps and floors. Make notes describing the views from windows and doors.

Don't be afraid to take photographs to help you visualize the garden during planning and design.

BASIC LANDSCAPE USES

Using the collected information, group together the various proposed functions and their related spaces into the four basic landscape categories: Public, Private, Family and Service Areas. Decide where they should be located on the site. This part of the process is very similar to designing the floor plan of a house.

Ensure that each group of uses relates logically to the others, and avoid conflicts. The final result should be functional and beautiful.

BASIC DESIGN PRINCIPLES

Certain basic principles should be appreciated by the garden planner.

Definition • Outdoor spaces and garden features should be defined. This may be achieved by a simple line at ground level, which may be the edge of a lawn or patio, a pathway, a hedge, a border or a row of trees, etc.

Enclosure • Outdoor spaces will often be enclosed, using hedges, borders of plants, walls, fences, screens, rows of trees, shrubs or flower beds. There is a relationship between definition and enclosure. By necessity, enclosure always creates definition but the reverse is not true. A line of bricks at ground level creates definition but not enclosure, whereas a hedge or wall creates both.

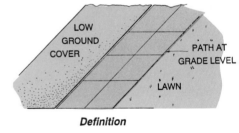

Definition

Circulation • Always provide logical, easy and comfortable circulation between and within the various spaces and features of a garden for people and, where appropriate, vehicles. Walkways, paths and driveways are important elements of garden development.

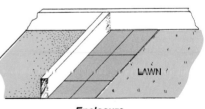

Enclosure

Utility and Beauty • Pursue the principle that good landscape planning and design is both functional and beautiful, and that these two objectives can be integrated.

PLACEMENT OF CROPS AND PLANTS

Here are a few practical considerations to consider when locating various crops, plants and features:

VEGETABLES

The site should be as level as possible, open and sunny, receiving at least 8 hours of direct sunlight each day during mid-summer, and it should be sheltered from prevailing winds. In the Toronto area, rows should run north and south. The area should be defined and preferably separated from the rest of the garden by a live or architectural screen.

TREE FRUITS

Avoid frost pockets such as low lying areas and river valley bottoms. They will grow in a wide range of soil types from sandy to clay loams. Good drainage is essential. Tree fruits may be grown on most sites except those facing north-west. Tender fruits such as apricots and peaches should be planted close to a south-east or west facing fence, wall or hedge. An orchard or fruit garden may be defined and screened from, or be visually integrated with, other areas of the garden, depending on the specific layout and the designer's intention and preference.

SOFT FRUITS

Most sites are suitable provided they are not invaded by tree root systems or shaded. Avoid frost pockets. Southeast to southwest facing locations are best. Select locations protected from prevailing winds by hedges, a house or natural bush.

TREES AND SHRUBS

Trees and shrubs may be used in a wide variety of locations depending on their individual preferences for aspect, sun and shade. Typical uses include:

• Single specimens in lawns, beds, borders, planters and planting holes in paved areas

• Small groups in beds and borders

• Groves to create naturalistic settings

• Plants widely spaced in lines to create tall, open intermittent screens and loose hedges; or lines closely spaced to create dense, tall and medium hedges

• Trees or shrubs as components of windbreaks.

The following factors should be taken into account when planning the placement of trees and shrubs:

Size at Maturity • Sufficient space must be provided to allow woody plants to grow and achieve mature size and the designer's intended effect. Find out the expected height and spread at maturity. See *Chapter 8*, Size and Form.

Form • Woody plants have a characteristic shape or form which may be similar throughout the life of a plant or change with its age.

Texture • This is largely determined by the density of the branch, twig structure and size of leaves. Plants with widely spaced, large leaves are said to be "coarse" textured, while those with densely distributed, small leaves are described as "fine" textured.

Foliage Colour • Summer foliage colour is an important long-term design value. Frequently seen colours include reddish-purple, yellow, silvery or grey, and variegated white or yellow.

Flowers • Colour, form, texture and time of flowering are important considerations.

Bark • Bark is an important element of colour and texture, particularly during winter.

Fruit • Fruit adds a source of colour in late summer, autumn and early winter.

Autumn Colour • Trees and shrubs can provide a final blaze of colour at the close of the growing season.

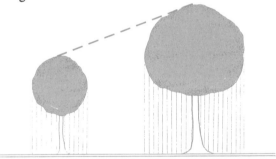

Trees Increase in Size and Spread over Time.

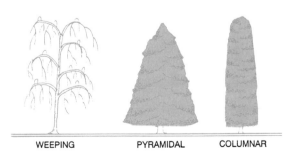

WEEPING   PYRAMIDAL   COLUMNAR

Tree Size and Forms

HERBACEOUS PERENNIALS

Herbaceous perennials may be planted alone or mixed with shrubs and annuals in beds, borders, and planters.

- The classic "herbaceous border," which contains a wide variety of herbaceous perennials and sometimes annuals, particularly towards the front. Variations on the theme include spring and fall flowering borders and those featuring specific colour schemes such as purple-mauve flowers, white flowers and silvery foliage.
- Combinations of perennials with shrubs and annuals in mixed borders.
- Shade-loving and shade-tolerant combinations, which are very appropriate and attractive in woodland gardens and shady areas.
- The use of perennials as excellent summer ground covers.

Except for shade-loving and shade-tolerant types, most herbaceous perennials prefer open, sunny locations, protected from wind. Open, gentle, north-facing slopes, protected from winter winds, make excellent environments. Locations on the north side of a house, fence or wall, just beyond the areas shaded during mid-summer, are also good spots.

As discussed with trees and shrubs — size, form, texture, foliage colour, flower colour and timing are important in the selection of perennials.

ANNUALS

Annuals are unique since, aside from plants with coloured foliage, they provide the longest period of colour during the growing season. Like herbaceous perennials, annuals may be used in a variety of ways in both sunny and shady locations they provide splashes and highlights of strong, bright, long-term colour. In addition to beds and borders, plant them in pots, urns, tubs and planters.

Design characteristics for annuals are similar to those for other plants. However, due to their strong colours and the common practice of close spacing and massed planting, height and colour of annuals are the major design considerations.

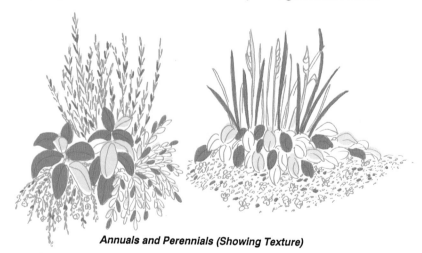

Annuals and Perennials (Showing Texture)

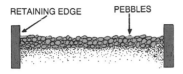

Inert Ground Cover on Compact Soil

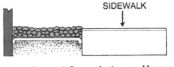

Inert Ground Cover between House and Sidewalk

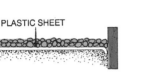

Inert Ground Cover on a Plastic Sheet

Inert Ground Cover with Plant

GROUND COVERS

As the name suggests, these are plants or inert materials that cover the surface of the ground. Ground covering plants include a wide range of evergreen and deciduous shrubs, as well as herbaceous perennials and annuals. Inert ground covers include gravel, shale, pebbles, crushed rock, marble chips, bark and so on, which are placed directly on the ground, on landscape fabrics or on perforated plastic sheets.

Inert ground covers are used: where it is difficult or impossible to grow plants; in areas of high traffic; to deliberately reduce or minimize the use of plants and thereby, maintenance; to create surfaces of interesting colour and texture, contrasting or harmonizing with lawns, decks, paved areas and other surfaces; and as mulches for live plantings.

In addition to some of the above uses, live covers are also used: to link groups of shrubs and perennials in planting arrangements; to create interesting live carpets and tapestries using texture, colour and form; to cover areas where grass will not grow; to cover slopes, banks, mounds, oddly shaped areas and shady places where mowing and other maintenance is difficult.

Planting on Slopes
Unless special provisions are made for irrigation and surface soil stabilization, the maximum recommended slope for a "planted bank" is just over one vertical to two horizontal, or a 30% grade.

VINES

Depending on their individual characteristics, vines may be used as climbers, trailers or ground covers. Climbers and trailers will climb up or trail over and down walls, fences, slopes, trees and shrubs, pillars, pergolas, trellises and other supports. Screens of various densities can be developed and less attractive features hidden.

Vines are excellent for creating vertical accents and delicate traceries on walls, fences, screens and arches, providing interesting and welcome contrasts of form.

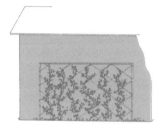 

BULBS, CORMS AND TUBERS

Many kinds of hardy and tender plants with underground bulbs, corms, tubers and tuberous roots may be grown, adding to the gardener's palette. For planning and design purposes they may be considered in the same light as herbaceous perennials and annuals. However, several kinds have additional, significant characteristics: some flower early or late in the season, and others are upright or arching, with sword shaped, grass-like or narrow foliage, resulting in strong or distinctive landscape forms.

LAWNS

Most lawns require an open, sunny location. If lawns are desired in shaded areas, shade-tolerant grasses must be selected.

When locating a lawn on a site, bear in mind that the minimum surface slope should rise or fall 1 unit vertically over 100 units horizontally on well drained soils and 2 in 100 on poorly drained soils. Avoid slopes greater than 15 in 100. The maximum "mowable" slope is 1 in 3. On slopes that are too steep to mow, the development of terraces is strongly recommended. Wherever possible, use terraces to take advantage of differences in elevation to add visual interest to a landscape. In addition to forming the basic carpet in a garden, lawns provide a verdant background and a universal foil to all garden features and plants.

PLACEMENT OF ARCHITECTURAL FEATURES

It is unlikely that any urban garden can be satisfactorily developed without some "hard landscape" and architectural features. While pathways, driveways, front and back steps, and paved patios are commonly included, less obvious features are often overlooked. Here are a few.

TERRACES AND DECKS

Terraced lawns have been previously mentioned. Paved terraces, retained by walls or linked by slopes to lawns, other paved areas or borders are very functional, interesting and beautiful features.

WALLS

These strong elements of design may be: tall walls, providing a strong sense of enclosure, protection and warmth; retaining walls of various sizes, holding back the soil or supporting terraces; walls of smaller stature, used to define garden spaces and planting areas; open-top walls, used as planters in their own right.

SCREENS, FENCES, TRELLISES, PERGOLAS AND ARCHES

All of these architectural features may be used to define and enclose garden spaces, paths, driveways and features, and to support plants.

STEPS

These are an often neglected element in the garden, yet they represent golden opportunities for creating beautiful design features. There are endless possible variations when using steps to bridge differences in elevation.

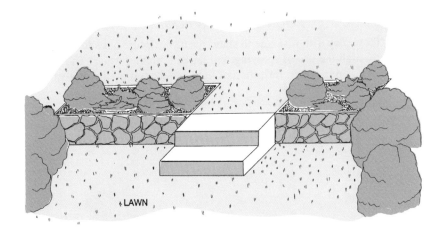

PAVED AREAS

In addition to the traditional concrete and interlocking bricks, there are many interesting and beautiful paving materials available, including gravel, crushed rock, shale, asphalt, bricks, natural and manufactured paving blocks, wooden blocks, cross-sections of tree trunks, and several proprietary products.

Don't forget that besides the customary "patio," to accommodate chairs, tables and a barbecue, there are other outdoor spaces, particularly those receiving hard pedestrian use, where paving makes good sense.

STATUARY, SCULPTURE, AND STONE FEATURES

These elements can add much interest, beauty and variety of form to a garden. As points of interest or focal points to terminate vistas, paths and strong lines of sight, they play an important role in garden design and exterior decoration. They are also very attractive when associated with walls, paved areas and lawns.

GAZEBOS AND SUMMER HOUSES

These are attractive and functional additions to a garden, and are very useful for outdoor entertaining and shelter in wet weather.

GREENHOUSES

If you plan to have a greenhouse eventually, be sure to provide space for it in a location where there will be plenty of unobstructed sunlight. Locate it in relation to the other service functions in the garden, unless you plan to use it as an architectural feature.

SHEDS

These are very useful for storing lawn mowers, tools, garden furniture, fertilizers and so on. Even if you don't plan to build immediately, location and space should be indicated on the original plan.

FOUNTAINS AND POOLS

Visually, these play a similar role to statuary and sculpture but add the value of movement through the use of spraying, falling and running water. The sound of rippling and splashing water, reflection of light and the tranquility of a still pool, provide additional dimensions.

In addition to the kinds of functional outdoor spaces or rooms previously described, bear in mind when planning that for the specialist, hobbyist and general gardening enthusiast, there are several types of garden that may be specially featured as a part of a larger garden or even may be used as its general theme.

ROCK GARDENS

These require open, sunny locations, exposed to the south or southwest, away from the roots and overhanging canopies of trees. While gentle slopes are ideal, with careful design and construction, flat areas can be satisfactory. Perfect drainage is a must.

WATER AND BOG GARDENS

Usually less formal than pools, these can be naturalistic ponds and streams, and can include waterfalls of various scales, with related marginal and wetland areas. They require sunny to light, semi-shaded locations but not heavily shaded areas. If streams are to be featured, slightly sloping land is the easiest to develop. Streams, pools and bogs associate well with rock gardens, if drainage for the latter is not compromised.

WOODLAND GARDENS

These types of gardens provide naturalistic woodland settings, containing sunny, semi-shaded, and more heavily shaded areas to accommodate a wide variety of plants, many of which prefer a more or less shady environment.

An ideal site will be naturally wooded or contain an adequate number of more or less mature planted trees, and provide a variety of micro-environments. There should be sufficient trees to allow immediate plantings of woodland plants. Interplanting with new trees will facilitate the development of additional, future environments.

WILD GARDENS

Very appealing gardens approaching wild landscapes can be created with minimal land development. They may contain elements of rock, water, bog and woodland gardens. Meadows, marshes and prairies may comprise all or just a part of a wild garden.

Development is restricted to naturalistic paths, related access facilities, and plantings of native and allied, introduced plants, supplementing existing vegetation.

ENVIRONMENTAL CONTROL

While there is little that can be done to make significant, permanent changes to the climate, there are a few time-proven methods of achieving a degree of control and modification.

WIND

Windbreaks, walls, fences, screens, hedges, and shrub borders all help to break the force of wind. In general, the height of a screen determines the size of the area protected on the sheltered side (about twenty times its height). Density determines the pattern and degree of turbulence on the sheltered side. Wind screens that break the force of the wind but allow some to pass through are best. They provide a large area of protection with minimal turbulence problems.

TEMPERATURE

Wind screens also help to increase temperatures on their sheltered side. Radiant heat from walls, fences and paved areas can significantly increase temperatures near by. Temperatures can be lowered by shading the garden with trees, shrubs, walls or trellises. Water featurEs can cool the garden, but may also increase its humidity.

SUN AND SHADE

The garden planner should judge the angle and path of the sun in winter, summer, spring and fall. Exact information may be obtained from the local office of Environment Canada. Using this data, patterns of shade cast by existing and proposed live and architectural features can be plotted. This makes it possible to plan the location of sunny and shady areas; provide for protection from sun (for example in late evening, low angled sun may shine directly into the eyes of a person sitting on the patio); and determine the kinds of plants for various areas.

FROST PROTECTION

Avoid placing the fruit and vegetable gardens, early flowering and late maturing plants, and less hardy plants, in frost pockets. Frost pockets are low lying areas that collect and hold cold air. Always remember that cold air is heavier than warm, and flows downhill.

Beware of placing hedges that are densely twigged from top to bottom or solid fences across a slope. The cold air will build up and pool against the barrier. Always provide adequate openings in the barrier or at its base to allow for unimpeded flow of cold air down the slope.

NOISE CONTROL

Noise may be controlled by the same methods as wind. Solid protection, however, is best. While it may be romantic to believe that nature has provided us mortals with the ideal noise barrier in the form of trees, it really isn't so. While trees undoubtedly provide a measure of noise absorption and control, tall, solid walls do the best job.

ATTRACTING BIRDS

Once a garden reaches a reasonable level of maturity, local birds will naturally visit and often nest. This requires patience. For gardeners in a bit of a hurry or for those who wish to attract specific kinds of birds, here are a few ideas.

Plant evergreen and deciduous trees, and some densely twigged shrubs to provide a variety of nesting habitats. Provide a variety of nesting boxes that are appropriately designed to attract local or uncommon species. Use plants that produce abundant berries, nuts and seeds. Keep insect control to the minimum, nessary for the garden. Provide water for drinking and bathing. Establish feeding stations for resident species, particularly in winter.

You may wish to consult people in local wildlife associations for more specific and additional advice.

CHAPTER 3

BASIC SOIL IMPROVEMENT

Several techniques may be employed to improve soil conditions and thereby maximize the appearance and yield of your garden.

Gardeners who are interested in a quick review of the basic principles which underlie soil improvement may wish to read "The Background to Soil Improvement Practices," at the end of this chapter.

The best soils for gardening are loams, which are mixtures of clay, silt and sand. Composition ranges from 5% to 20% clay and from 20% to 60% sand, with silt making up the balance. For gardening purposes loams are described as "clayey," "silty" or "sandy", depending on which material predominates. The ideal, often elusive, "medium loam" is a soil not dominated by clay, silt or sand. Its mineral content is made up of approximately 20% clay, 40% silt, and 40% coarse sand, and includes a generous amount of organic matter and humus. Such a soil doesn't have the extreme characteristics of either clay or sand. It is well drained, easy to work and well aerated, containing adequate water and plenty of plant foods.

There are three fundamental techniques used to improve soils: drainage, tillage, and the addition of soil-improving materials.

DRAINAGE

Surface drainage is usually a function of the slope of the land. Provided the soil is permeable and overlies a well-drained subsoil, drainage is not normally a serious problem in most well planned and engineered urban subdivisions. However, where the top soil overlies an impervious subsoil or the subsoil itself is saturated, a drainage scheme may be needed.

Soils with high water tables are those which are continually wet, holding water for long periods after rain and snow thaw. Surface water takes a long time to drain away. Providing adequate drainage is the first step in soil improvement.

The fundamental principle of drainage is that water flows downhill and seeks its own level. Land drainage may involve one or more of three general techniques.

Collection • Removal of water, first involves collecting surplus water.

Transportation • The water must be transported away from the affected site.

Disposal • It must be then disposed of in a satisfactory manner.

There are several options for developing adequate drainage:

Digging • The gardener may dig one or two spits (spade-depths) into the ground to break impermeable soil layers or hard-pans and improve porosity. Where it is practical, this method may eliminate the collection step, and it facilitates transportation and disposal in an easy, downward manner.

Soakways • Soakways are large, deep holes lined with non-cemented bricks and filled with broken bricks, rubble and coarse gravel to within 45 - 60 cm of ground level. A layer of medium gravel is added, covered by tar paper or coarse peat, and then covered with top soil. These structures will drain the immediate, surrounding area, holding the water until it gradually drains away. They may also be used as a disposal pit for water transported from elsewhere.

Trenches • Another drainage option is gravel-filled trenches. Flat-bottomed trenches with sloping sides are dug approximately half a metre deep. Thirty centimetres of coarse gravel is placed in the bottom and covered with 20 to 30 cm of top soil. These constructions may act as mini-soakways, or serve to collect and transport water.

Tiles • Serious drainage problems may require agricultural tile drains laid in trenches, bedded on and covered with gravel, then covered with top soil. These collect and transport water to a lower-lying pond, creek, lake, dry well, ditch or other place for disposal.

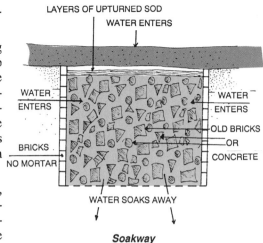

Soakway

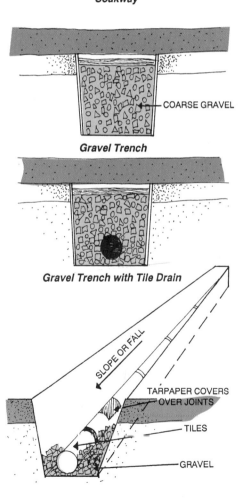

Gravel Trench

Gravel Trench with Tile Drain

The major method of soil improvement is to turn it over, and thoroughly mix it with materials such as organic matter, gritty materials and fertilizers. Single and double digging, can be readily adapted to the roto-tiller.

SINGLE DIGGING

The objective of single digging is to turn over and break up the soil, one spit deep, and thoroughly mix in the improvement materials.

As a simple example, digging a rectangular plot is described.

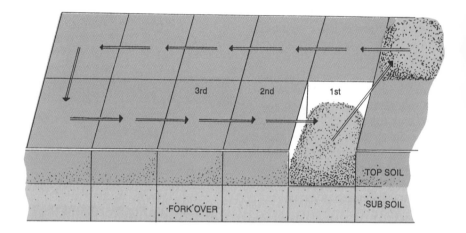

- Using a garden line, divide the plot into two equal halves — A and B.
- Mark a trench, 40 cm wide, across one end of Half A.
- Using a square-nosed garden spade, dig out the top soil a full spade's depth, leaving a straight-sided, flat-bottomed trench. Place excavated soil in a pile just outside the end of Half B.
- Mark a second 40 cm trench behind the first.
- Dig the soil from this second trench, throwing it forward to fill the first trench. Be sure that every crumb of soil is moved. Due to expansion, the soil in the trench will be higher than the surrounding land.
- Continue working backwards, down Half A, trench by trench until the end of the plot is reached.
- Take out the next trench, adjacent, on Half B, placing the soil into the last trench of Half A.
- Continue digging Half B, trench by trench as previously described.
- Fill in the final trench on Half B with the pile of soil dug from the first trench of Half A.

DOUBLE DIGGING

The objective of double digging is to turn over and break up the soil two spits deep, keeping the two spits, or top soil and subsoil, unmixed — leaving them in their respective horizons.

Although labour intensive, this is an excellent method for: breaking new ground, especially undisturbed pasture; initial preparation for permanent beds and borders of trees and shrubs, herbaceous perennials, fruits, asparagus and rhubarb; or breaking an impervious layer, hard-pan or badly drained subsoil below the top soil.

The general method is similar to single digging with the following changes:

• Use a 60 cm wide trench.

• After digging out the top soil, fork over and break up the bottom of the trench (subsoil) a spit deep, before turning over the top soil into it from the next trench.

On shallow top soils, double digging allows for the removal of some subsoil and its replacement with top soil. It may also be used to lower the elevation of an area by removing subsoil from under the topsoil.

Both methods of digging allow for the incorporation of organic matter. Simply spread the material over the soil surface prior to digging. Scatter it over the newly turned soil during digging, covering it with soil as work proceeds.

TIMING

The best time to dig is late fall. Soil can be turned over in large lumps which will be exposed to the beneficial cleansing and pulverizing effects of rain, snow and freeze and thaw cycles as winter progresses. Since most soils expand about 20 - 25% when dug, fall digging also allows the longest time for the soil to settle. This is particularly important when land is double dug. Furthermore, cool weather makes the task easier on the digger.

If you dig in spring, too late for natural settlement to occur, you may need to lightly consolidate the soil prior to planting or seeding. Walking on your heels over the soil, leaving closely spaced imprints, will do the job, as will one or two heavy waterings. When double digging, be sure to consolidate the lower spit after forking it over, before covering with top soil.

Never dig or cultivate soil when it is wet. This is of critical importance on clay-dominated soils. Compressing wet soil will destroy crumb structure, porosity, air holding capacity, and will impede local drainage.

SOIL AMENDMENTS

Several organic and inorganic materials may be used to improve soils.

ANIMAL MANURES

Bulky, fresh or near-fresh, strawy, farmyard or stable manures should not be used just prior to planting or seeding since they may burn roots. Heavy applications may be safely made on open land in late fall. For most uses, sweet-smelling, easily-crumbled, non-sticky, well-rotted manures may be safely applied at any time. Fresh but reasonably dry, crumbly and easy to handle, cow manure is an excellent source of organic matter. Sheep, chicken and pig manures are best when dried, crumbled and used as organic fertilizers during the growing season or to make liquid fertilizers.

COMPOST

Well-rotted, reasonably dry, non-slimy, crumbly-flaky compost is an excellent source of organic matter. Compost is discussed later in this chapter.

PEAT MOSS

Pure, granular, sterilized, fibrous, sphagnum peat, while containing few immediately available plant foods, is an excellent form of slow-decomposing, water retaining organic matter that has a long-term, beneficial effect on soil structure. It is a valuable additive in lawn construction and in the preparation of permanent plantings of trees, shrubs and herbaceous perennials. Since peat moss is a semi-raw form of organic matter, during its decomposition the soil organisms use much of the available nitrogen. It is therefore necessary to add a nitrogen fertilizer to the soil to compensate.

RAW ADDITIVES

Non-resinous, small-size wood chips and sawdust, chopped straw, hay and similar forms of raw organic matter may be used. Like peat moss, they break down slowly, using available nitrogen for which compensation must be made.

GREEN MANURES

Soil Testing
A variety of soil testing products, ranging from simple pH testers to elaborate nutrient analysis kits, may be purchased from garden centres. Contact your District Agriculturalist for information about soil testing services.

Leafy-green crops such as rye, mustard, rape, clovers and annual lupins may be sown, allowed to grow and then turned under just before flowering. Extra nitrogen is required with this system of soil improvement. Adequate time must be allowed for decomposition before planting or seeding takes place. This may be easily judged by digging up and examining the decomposing organic matter. Decomposition is accelerated if the crop is cut up using a rotary mower, prior to digging it in.

GRAVELS AND SANDS

Fine, washed gravels up to half a centimetre across and coarse, angular particle sands with most grains between 15 and 30 mm may be used to improve the porosity, drainage and structure of clay soils. These must be thoroughly mixed with the clay to be effective. Large quantities of these substances may be required to make a noticeable improvement in porosity and texture; keep in mind that an ideal loam contains about 20% clay and 40% coarse sand. Don't use round-particle sands unless they are very coarse. Beware of very fine builder's sands: when mixed with clay, an intractable form of concrete results.

VERMICULITE AND PERLITE

Although not commonly used outdoors, such products may be used to improve porosity and help lighten heavy soils, but they may prove expensive where large quantities are involved.

LIME

The addition of lime will reduce soil acidity or "sweeten" sour soils. It is mostly used in the forms of ground or powdered chalk, ground limestone and hydrated lime. Avoid the hot or caustic forms except when applying to open, uncropped land in the fall. Soil testing is the most dependable way to determine if a soil needs lime and if so, how much to add. In Southern Ontario, the pH of the soil is usually basic (above 7) and thus contains high calcium. Therefore, liming is not needed.

SULPHUR AND ALUMINUM SULPHATE

These chemicals are used to increase the acidity of soils. They should be used only after soil testing indicates a need for them.

Aluminum sulphate is also used to "blue" the flowers of the common, florist's hydrangea.

OTHER SOIL IMPROVEMENT PRACTICES

FORKING

A steel-tined digging fork is used to overturn lightly the top 8 to 15 cm of soil, to break down the lumps to a finer texture, and to mix in soil amendments. Forking is an important step to take prior to raking, when preparing a seed bed. A fork is also used to break up the soil surface between permanent plants in beds and borders, to aerate the soil and to mix in mulches and fertilizers.

RAKING

During the preparation of a seed or transplanting bed, use a steel rake to break down the top five to ten centimetres of soil surface into small granules. A rake is also used to gather and remove stones and debris from the soil's surface.

HOEING

Use a hoe to break the soil crust and develop a shallow layer of fine soil or dust mulch. This will reduce water loss through evaporation.

A hoe is also used to chop off weeds just below soil level, to cultivate shallowly, and to draw soil or "earth up" around the bases of plants.

MULCHING

Mulching involves the application of a shallow layer of organic matter to the soil surface. This conserves moisture, keeps the soil cool, and smothers weeds, preventing their germination. Mulching also provides a mild feed. When forked into the soil, the mulch increases the organic matter content.

WATERING

The amount of water required by root systems varies with the kind of plant and the environment. The general guideline is to water slowly and copiously, penetrating the soil deeply, when needed, but leaving as long an interval as is practical between waterings. This will encourage deep rooting and drought-tolerance in plants.

The main deviation from this procedure occurs when seeds are sown and germinating. Rows of seeds, seed beds and newly sown lawns should be watered frequently and lightly with shallow penetration, taking care not to disturb soil surfaces until germination has occurred. After the seeds have sprouted, you can gradually increase the amount of water per application and decrease the frequency of application, until the general guideline is attained.

Seedbed Preparation
Dig, and if required manure the plot. If fall digging is practised, the addition of fertilizer is left until spring. Fork over the plot to break down lumps, and mix in the manure and fertilizer. Finally, rake and cross-rake to develop a level, 4 to 5 cm deep, surface layer of fine granules.

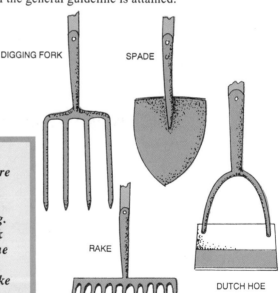

DIGGING FORK   SPADE

RAKE

DUTCH HOE

Garden Implements

FERTILIZERS

Fertilizers are used to supply foods to plants. There are two classes of fertilizer: organic fertilizers which are derived from animal and vegetable sources, and inorganic or so-called "chemical" fertilizers.

Since plants take up food in inorganic forms, it makes little if any difference to the plants whether the foods are derived from organic or inorganic fertilizers. The only advantages to using organic fertilizers is that they generally release nutrients slowly over a longer period, eventually adding to the humus content of the soil. Disadvantages include a possible low nutrient content, high unit cost and a slow release of nutrients.

Nitrogen (N), phosphorous (P) and potassium (K) are the most common foods in most fertilizers. By law, the percentage of these foods must be stated on the package. They are expressed as three numbers connected with hyphens. If the package is labelled 10-30-10, for example, it means that the fertilizer contains 10%N, 30%P and 10%K. The numbers always represent N, P, and K, in that order.

Unit analysis compares the cost per unit of a specific food in different fertilizers. The method is to divide the cost of each fertilizer being compared by the percentage of respective foods it contains. As a hypothetical example, let us look at the unit cost of N in three fertilizers. 10-30-10 @ $30/50 kg has a unit cost of $30/10 or $3.00. The unit cost of 16-20-0 @ $40 is $2.50 and 33-0-0 @ $50 is $1.52. Therefore although the cost per 50 kg of 33-0-0 is highest, its cost per unit of N is lowest.

APPLICATION

Rates of application of fertilizer vary with the crop and purpose. See specific chapters for detailed information, or follow directions on the package.

The most common method of application is broadcasting, which involves spreading fertilizer on the soil's surface. In the cultivation of vegetables, application in or to the sides of seed rows is sometimes recommended. Water-soluble fertilizers may be applied directly to the root zones of plants and, in the case of those kinds absorbed through the leaves, directly to the foliage.

To avoid burning foliage during or following application of dry fertilizers:
- *apply at the recommended rate*
- *spread evenly and uniformly over the soil surface or lown*
- *unless you are using a liquid foliar fertilizer, don't apply to leaves unless it is immediately washed off by water*
- *apply to moist soil*
- *don't apply to wet foliage*
- *water after application*

COMPOSTING

Well-rotted garden refuse is a valuable source of excellent, low-cost, organic matter. Just about any material of vegetable origin can be used as long as it's not too woody. Compost may be used as a soil amendment or as a mulch. Several compact forms of compost container systems are available. Traditional methods are open heaps and side-by-side double containers, usually made of wood. The production of well-rotted, granular, non-slimy, sweet smelling compost is accomplished by aerobic decomposition which requires oxygen, water and the appropriate oxygen-breathing bacteria. The fundamental method proceeds as follows:

- establish a level, well drained site where surplus water can run away from the bottom of the compost heap
- spread the different kinds of raw organic matter in even layers of uniform depth
- create a maximum heap-height of two metres
- sprinkle each third of a metre's depth of material with water and a high nitrogen (liquid or dry) fertilizer
- after building to full height, allow the heap to settle to approximately one half its height
- starting at one end of the heap, use a fork to turn it over, moving the composting materials about half a metre to the left or right
- during turn-over, loosen any compacted material and water dry spots
- re-shape and tidy the heap
- again allow the heap to settle, then turn it over and reshape
- When using a double-bin technique, the compost is turned from bin to bin two or more times, depending on the rate of decomposition

Some gardeners place a few evenly spaced layers of top soil through the heap. These inject bacteria and accelerate decomposition.

The introduction of 8-cm-deep layers of fresh, strawy stable or barnyard manure every 30 - 40 cm will also hasten decomposition and enrich the resulting compost. However a temporary unpleasant smell may be a negative feature of this option.

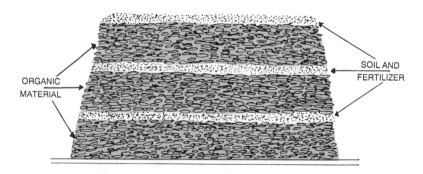

SOIL AND FERTILIZER

ORGANIC MATERIAL

Building a Compost Heap

Shallow, even-depth layers of grass clippings are a useful addition to composts. Allow the clippings to wilt before placing them on the heap. Grass should not be used within 48 hours of having been sprayed with lawn herbicide.

In the Toronto area, it takes 6 to 12 months to make good compost.

THE BACKGROUND TO SOIL IMPROVEMENT

FOOD SOURCES FOR PLANTS

Plants obtain their nutrients from two basic sources: the atmosphere and the soil.

Atmosphere • Atmospheric carbon dioxide is used in photosynthesis, the process by which plants manufacture simple sugars using energy from sunlight and the catalytic properties of chlorophyll. Respiration, the reverse of photosynthesis, uses oxygen to burn or break down simple sugars, thereby releasing stored energy from the sun and making it available for growth.

Soil Water • Hydrogen and oxygen are obtained from soil water and used in both photosynthesis and respiration.

Soil • All other plant foods are obtained from the soil, including nitrogen and sulphur which are essential in the formation of proteins. Hence, soil improvement is critically important as it increases fertility and makes soil-borne nutrients readily available to plants.

ESSENTIAL PLANT FOODS

While about 60 chemical elements have been found in plants, only 16 are generally considered to be essential for healthy growth. They are classified as macro and micro nutrients, based on the amounts the plants use.

Macro nutrients include carbon, oxygen and hydrogen (obtained from air and water) and nitrogen, phosphorous, potassium, sulphur, magnesium and calcium (obtained from the soil).

Micro nutrients contained in the soil include chlorine, boron, iron, manganese, zinc, copper and molybdenum. Since very small amounts are required and many naturally occurring soils contain them in adequate quantities, they are generally available to plants. When specific shortages occur, they may be added to the soil or fed to plants in a suitable chemical form.

The three soil-borne foods of greatest concern to most gardeners, because they are required in the largest amounts, are nitrogen, phosphorous and potassium.

Nitrogen is an essential constituent of protein. It helps to produce a healthy, lush growth of new shoots and leaves, and promotes a dark green colour.

Phosphorous promotes the development of strong, healthy root systems, the setting of shoot and flower buds and the quality of flowers and seeds.

Potassium is involved in the development of the mechanical strength of stems and roots, and resistance to diseases.

Other macro nutrients required in smaller amounts include sulphur which promotes rich green colour; calcium, which glues plant cells together; and iron and magnesium, both required for the development of chlorophyll, which makes possible the process of photosynthesis and the production of sugar.

SOIL COMPOSITION

Most soils are made up of five basic components: minerals, organic matter, water, air and soil organisms.

Minerals • In gardeners' terms, the mineral component of soils include clay, sand and silt.

Clay is made up of very tiny, in some cases microscopic, mineral particles. These are flat and very tightly packed. Due to the huge combined surface area of the particles, they hold a lot of water. While cold, wet and difficult to cultivate, clays contain plenty of plant foods. They also combine with humus, derived from organic matter, to form the chemically active, food producing clay-humus colloids. (See "Organic Matter", below).

Sands comprise large, rough, uneven, sometimes rounded particles. They hold little water and drain quickly. Manures and other forms of organic matter are quickly used up in sands, which generally contain small quantities of plant foods and are not very fertile. However, because of their loose structures, they are easy to work.

Silt particles are larger than those of clay but smaller than sand particles. They are also intermediate in their qualities, which vary with particle size. When fine, silts can be wet and sticky; when coarse, they are well drained and dry. Silts are often mixed with fine sands.

Organic Matter • Organic matter is made up of the decomposing remains of plants and animals. This is broken down by insects, fungi and bacteria to form humus, a formless, dark brown to blackish substance which is the end product of decomposition. During the process, plant foods are returned to the soil, enriching it and increasing fertility. Carbon dioxide is also produced and it combines with water to form mild carbonic acid, which breaks down minerals, thereby releasing plant foods.

In sandy soils, humus helps to bind the loose particles into firmer aggregates and retains water, acting as a sponge. When mixed with clay, humus opens up the soil by separating particles, improving porosity and drainage, and by helping to develop aggregates of soil particles it improves workability. It also helps form clay-humus colloids which enhance the availability of plant foods and fertility.

A Comparison of Clay and Sand
Silts will fall somewhere in between, depending on their particle size.

	Clay Soils	Sandy Soils
Cultivation	Heavy	Light
Water Content	Wet	Dry
Temperature	Cold	Warm
Spring Warm-up	Late	Early
Food Content	Rich	Poor
Food Availability	Unwilling	Willing
Holding Power	Miserly	Spendthrift

Soil Water • A mixture of water, weak carbonic acid and dissolved plant foods is contained in the spaces between soil particles and forms a film around the particles. Soil water exists in two states: "unavailable" water is tightly bound to the particles and is not accessible by the plant roots; "available" water, on the other hand, is usable by plants. It is "available" water which is of most interest to gardeners.

Soil Air • Oxygen, hydrogen, carbon dioxide and other atmospheric gases are contained in the spaces between soil particles. As mentioned earlier, oxygen is required by plants for respiration, and carbon dioxide is dissolved in water to form carbonic acid which helps release nutrients from soil minerals. In water-logged soils where oxygen is excluded from the air spaces, asphyxiation of the roots may occur.

Soil Organisms • A variety of small mammals, insects, worms, mollusks, protozoa, fungi and bacteria inhabit fertile soils. Through their feeding, digesting and eliminating activities they break down organic matter, resulting in humus formation and the release of plant foods. They are essential to the decomposition of organic matter and humus formation which enriches the soil.

Fertile soils contain an abundance of micro-organisms which are dependent on adequate organic matter for their survival. There is therefore a reciprocal relationship between organic matter, biological activity and fertility.

CHAPTER 4

GARDENING IN SMALL SPACES

This chapter is aimed at the urban gardener who doesn't have an abundance of space. "Small spaces" include townhouse, courtyard and balcony gardens.

Plants in such gardens may be grown in smaller versions of the ground level beds and borders used in larger urban gardens. Raised planting areas, planters and various kinds of containers are characteristic features. Gardening on apartment balconies is usually restricted exclusively to growing plants in containers.

Due to space limitations, planning should be carried out with considerable care. For general planning considerations, see *Chapter 2*. Special planning requirements will be mentioned as appropriate.

Annuals for Planters

In the Sun	*In the Shade*	*Dwarf Nasturtium*
		Edging Lobelia
Annual Pink	*Annual Vinca*	*Fuchsia*
Baby's-breath	*Browallia*	*Ivy-leaved Geranium*
Cape Marigold	*Coleus*	*Lantana*
Cockscomb	*Edging Lobelia*	*Mexican Cigar Plant*
Cornflower	*Impatience*	*Pendulus Begonia*
Dusty Miller	*Pansy*	
Dwarf Snapdragon	*Wax Begonia*	*Accent or Focal Point*
Flossflower		
Geranium	*Trailers or Climbers*	*Canna Lily*
Ice Plant	*(May also be used*	*Dracaena Spike*
Marigolds	*in hanging baskets)*	*Fountain Grass*
Moss Rose		*Pampas Grass*
Nasturtium	*Black-eyed Susan Vine*	*Standard Fuchsia*
Petunia	*Cape Marigold*	*Standard Heliotrope*
Scarlet Sage	*Cascade-type Petunia*	*Standard Lantana*
Sweet Alyssum	*Cup-and-Saucer Vine*	
Zinnias	*Dwarf Morning Glory*	

PLANTERS AND CONTAINERS

These are distinctive features of small gardens.

PLANTERS

These more or less permanent, fixed planting areas of many small landscapes impart a basic sense of design. Not likely to be found on balconies, they include:

• grade-level holes of various shapes and sizes, cut into paved and grass areas
• peripheral and other borders at ground level
• raised, wall-retained planting areas and borders of various shapes and heights
• open-top planter walls
• large containers, too heavy to move frequently

CONTAINERS

Portable boxes, dishes, pots, vases and urns may be used. They can be made of wood, concrete, baked clay, plastic or ceramic materials. Containers are available in a wide range of designs and materials, from simple clay and terra-cotta flower pots to large concrete boxes, to elaborate Grecian urns made of stone.

For growing vegetables, particularly on balconies, small wooden boxes are ideal since they can be moved without heroic measures. When several are carefully arranged and planted, significant production may be achieved. A practical box size is 120 cm long, 40 cm wide and 30 cm deep. The box should sit on two 5 x 10 cm runners to keep it off the ground, thereby ensuring adequate drainage and preventing rot. Use 2 cm particle board or plywood, treated with a non-petroleum based wood preservative, and lined with a 4 mm polyethylene film.

Window boxes are available in wood, plastic and metal. In addition to gracing windows, they may be used along the sides of railings and fences, on top of fences and screens, and as low planters in a variety of settings.

DRAINAGE

It is important that surplus water can freely drain out of planters and containers. As long as containers have an unobstructed drainage hole in the bottom — covered by a wire or plastic mesh screen, broken crocks or coarse gravel — impeded drainage is not likely to be a problem, even in the larger units. If the underlying soil is well drained, open-bottom planters should not be a problem. Solid-bottom planters should have drainage holes. In large, solid-bottom planters, over 60 cm deep, place a layer of coarse gravel in the bottom before filling with soil.

SOILS

For ground level and raised open-bottom planters, well-worked, medium loam, garden soil will be satisfactory for most plants.

For solid-bottom planters and containers, use a soil mix comprised by bulk of: 7 parts medium to heavy loam; 3 parts sterile, granular, fibrous, peat moss; 2 parts coarse, washed, angular particle sand with most particles between 15 and 30 mm across. Add 85 g of powdered chalk and 170 g of 5-10-5 fertilizer to each half cubic metre of compost. Omit the chalk if plants that need acid soil are to be grown. On balconies, the weight of this compost may be reduced by using perlite or vermiculite instead of sand.

"Cornell type" mix is a popular, light-weight, medium comprising equal parts of sterilized, granular peat moss and #4 grade vermiculite. To each 70 dm³ of mix, add and mix in thoroughly 150 ml of ground limestone, 75 ml of saltpetre and 4.5 L of warm water.

When mixing any compost, the peat moss must first be thoroughly moistened. Mix the peat and sand or vermiculite. Mix in the water to moisten. Finally mix in the loam and/or fertilizers.

Before filling a container, cover the drainage holes with pieces of 30 mm galvanized wire or plastic mesh to prevent soil mix from running out. When using a heavy soil mix in containers over 25 cm deep, place a 3 cm layer of peat moss or styrofoam balls, pellets or chips over the bottom prior to filling. Fill with soil mix, lightly compacting each 10 cm layer with the fingers. Leave a 2 cm deep watering space between the soil surface and the container rim. Using a watering can or hose with a spray head, water thoroughly to settle the soil.

WATERING

Due to the smaller volumes of soil in planters and containers, combined with faster drainage as a result of being raised above ground level, watering will generally be needed more frequently than in garden beds, especially in hot dry weather. Containers on balconies are particularly vulnerable, drying out quickly and regularly. If you are frequently absent, consider trickle irrigation and wick watering systems.

FERTILIZING

As a result of a smaller soil volume in small planters and containers, the amount and frequency of fertilizing will be increased, particularly for container-grown vegetables, annuals and other bedding plants. Vigorous herbaceous perennials and ground covers in smaller raised planters will need the same careful attention to fertilizing. On the other hand, it may be necessary to reduce the amount of fertilizer for small trees and larger shrubs to restrict their rate of growth. Dwarf shrubs will require restricted fertilizing. Trees and shrubs in grade level, open borders should be treated as in any other garden setting, requiring fertilizing once each spring.

MULCHING

In late spring or early summer, a 5 cm layer of well rotted manure or compost evenly spread over the soil surface between plants will help to retain soil water, keep the soil cool, provide a mild feed and suppress annual weeds. When forked into the soil each year in late fall, it will continually replenish the content of organic matter.

PLANT SELECTION

Although an occasional, carefully-located, larger specimen tree or shrub may be permitted in the larger small garden, as a general rule most plants will be of naturally small or dwarf stature, slow growing, or well adapted to restrictive pruning and clipping.

Plants with narrow-upright, columnar, pyramidal, and other strong or geometric forms are particularly useful and eye-appealing in small spaces.

Non-invasive ground covers may be used to link together groups of taller plants and to carpet parts of the garden floor, cover slopes and mounds, create interesting horizontal tapestries and prevent weeds.

Climbing plants are excellent in the small garden. They may be trained to climb up or cascade down walls, fences, screens, pillars, poles, trellises, pergolas and slopes. Climbers can provide delicate vertical tracery or dense screens of foliage, and strong vertical accents, without using much space at ground level.

Non-climbing shrubs suitable for training against walls, screens and fences are also very useful since they require less space than those allowed to grow naturally in the open.

Fruit may be grown using restricted forms of trees such as cordons, espaliers, fans and dwarf pyramids.

Winter Protection
In the Metro Toronto area, special winter protection for plants grown permanently in raised beds and containers is not generally required. Should winter survival problems be encountered, snow may be piled round the outside of planters and containers to provide exterior insulation. Fibreglass battens and bales of straw may also be used.

Generally, perennials will be non-invasive kinds with compact crowns and tufted habits. Plants with upright growth, strong form and interesting foliage are suitable candidates.

A wide range of annuals may be used, concentrating on small, dwarf and carpeting kinds, although occasional use of taller kinds as accent plants may be appropriate.

Plants that originate from bulbs, corms and tubers, especially those of dwarf stature and upright or pendulous habit can be used to enrich the small garden throughout the growing season.

PRUNING TREES AND SHRUBS

Bear in mind that a plant's root environment will affect its rate of shoot growth and, therefore, pruning practices. Those planted in open, ground-level beds and borders and larger, open-bottom, raised containers will generally produce more shoot growth than plants in solid-bottom, raised planters and containers.

In general, pruning practices will be similar to those used in gardens of a larger size. See Chapter 8, Trees and Shrubs for additional information.

Each year during the dormant period, all trees and shrubs should be checked. Where appropriate, normal form and maintenance pruning should be carried out. Special techniques that apply to small spaces include the following:

• During the dormant period — that is, before any sign of new growth — non-climbing, woody plants trained against walls, fences and screens should have overcrowded shoots thinned, long unbranched shoots shortened and very vigorous, unruly shoots completely removed back to their point of origin on major framework branches and trunks.

• Non-climbing, woody plants trained against walls, trellises and so on that flower earlier in the year on the previous year's shoots, should have all flowered shoots cut back to one or two buds beyond their points of origin on the permanent, mature branches which are trained to the wall or fence. This pruning should be carried out immediately after the flowers have faded.

• Such plants trained against walls or fences that bloom on the current year's shoots should have last year's flowered shoots cut back to one or two buds beyond their point of origin. Carry out this work in late winter or early spring while plants are completely dormant.

• Woody plants kept small by restrictive pruning (including restricted forms of fruit trees) should be subject to normal form and maintenance pruning before spring growth begins. However, they may also be pruned at the end of the third week in July by shortening all side shoots produced from the framework branches during the current year to three or four leaves beyond their point of origin on framework branches.

GROWING VEGETABLES

The economics of small garden production, using containers, is not the same as production at ground level. Scale is smaller but productivity may be higher, and costs may also be higher since the growing environment must first be constructed.

Cost of construction depends on standards selected. Manufactured containers cost more than do-it-yourself varieties, which in turn cost more than containers formerly used for other purposes.

One possible home-made container. It starts with a 2 cm particle board box, nailed, glued, painted and lined with 4 mm polyethylene film. The box is 1.2 m long, 40 cm wide and 30 cm deep, and it sits on two 5 x 5 cm runners. It holds:

• two 40 cm rows of bunching onions, sown at the ends;

• 12 station-sown leaf or small head lettuce, spaced 20 cm apart and 10 cm in from the sides;

• 3 single-stem tomatoes, planted 40 cm apart down the middle.

Onions and lettuce are sown April 20. Tomatoes are planted May 20 and covered with hot caps.

Yield is estimated at 6 bunches of onions, twelve 20 cm heads of lettuce and 7 to 8 kg of tomatoes.

Market value is calculated as follows:

Onions	6 @.40	$ 2.40
Lettuce	12 @.75	$ 9.00
Tomatoes	15-18 @.80	$ 12.00- $14.40
TOTAL		**$ 23.40- $25.80**

Estimated costs, not including labour, are:

Container	$ 7.50
Soil mix	11.00
Fertilizer	3.00
Water	2.00
Stakes	1.50
Seeds and plants	4.50
TOTAL	**$ 29.50**

Assuming the container has a life of 5 years and soil improvement costs $2.00 per year, the average annual cost for five years is $17.00.

Using the low yield figures, a saving of $ 6.40 would be realized. This represents a 37.6% return on investment over 120 days or an annualized return of 114%. Not a bad deal. But of course the real attraction is the improved flavour, convenience and satisfaction of growing your own crops.

All kinds of vegetables may be successfully grown in containers. Traditional window boxes with inside dimensions of 25 cm wide and 20 cm deep, of any convenient, easily handled lengths are also suitable for salad and root vegetables, as well as for annual flowers. Various shaped containers, approximately 30 x 30 cm and 25 cm deep, can hold single plants needing large soil volumes and lots of room, including cucumber, tomato, zucchini, eggplant and pepper.

ARCHITECTURAL FEATURES

Walls, fences, screens, trellises, pergolas, arches, pillars, statuary, sculpture, stone work, pools and fountains are particularly appropriate in smaller gardens. All form strong, permanent vertical accents, providing high visual appeal and interest without using much space at ground level. See *Chapter 2* for additional information.

BALCONIES

There are a few inherent restrictions in the development of balcony gardens:

- Access must be considered. All lumber, boxes, soil and plants must be carried up and down stairs, around landings, into elevators and/or through patio doors and windows.

- Weight is an important factor. A balcony must be able to support containers, soil and water, plus the gardener and friends. Generally, the safest place for the heaviest items is next to the building walls, but check with the building owner to be sure. If in doubt about the structural strength of a balcony, have it checked by an engineer.

- Water will be needed and an outdoor faucet is ideal. However, a light-weight plastic hose can easily be attached to a kitchen faucet. Trickle irrigation and wick watering are particularly appropriate.

- Drainage is a related problem. Ensure that drainage water follows the balcony's built-in path for shedding rainwater, to minimize drip problems for people below.

- Ensure that items can't roll, or be blown, off the balcony, endangering people below.

- Protect building walls and balcony floors, particularly those made of wood, from contact with soil and water. Place a 4 to 6 mm sheet of polyethylene between soil and building surfaces.

- Place the bases of containers on bricks or blocks, raising them above the floor to ensure good drainage and prevent rot.

- Consider scale, and don't use all available space for gardening. Plan carefully, leaving enough space for working, entertaining and sitting out.

THE MICRO CLIMATE

Gardening above ground level presents the challenge of a new environment. The closer a balcony is to the sun, the higher the light intensity. However, this is often modified. Balconies may be shaded by adjacent buildings, trees, enclosures and other balconies. Aspect is also important. South- and southwest-facing balconies receive the most direct light. East-facing balconies get sun from early morning until approximately noon; west-facing from noon until evening. Except in the early morning and late evening during summer, north-facing locations receive little direct sun but, when unobstructed, are reasonably light on bright days. Most balconies tend to be shadier next to the building wall than at the railings.

So many variables affect direct sunlight and light intensity, observe the degree of light penetration and patterns on the balcony. Make an inventory of sunny and shady spots, noting duration and time of day and year. Determine where light intensity can be increased by reflection. Paint walls white, or install reflector boards and mirrors. Replace solid enclosures with open railings, clear plastic or heavy glass. If practical, remove nearby trees.

On warm sunny balconies it may be necessary to provide for cooling shade. Blinds, curtains, screens and trellises may be used. Wind is a special problem, particularly on the upper balconies of high-rise apartments. The higher the balcony, the stronger the wind tends to be. Provide protection by using trellises, baffles and screens. Some enthusiasts use clear plastic or heavy glass. Secure taller plants by tying them to walls, railings, trellises, nets, poles and stakes.

Soils in containers dry out very quickly — a problem compounded if the gardener must be away. On a balcony, watering delayed may be the equivalent of watering denied, and early crop demise may be the result. Trickle irrigation and wick watering systems should be considered to alleviate the problem.

USE OF VERTICAL SPACE

Using strong brackets, clamps and other fasteners, smaller flower boxes may be attached to railings and walls. Depending on available light and vertical space, they may be arranged on more than one level. Unless special drainage arrangements have been made, hang flower boxes and baskets inside the railings and not over the street. Arrange containers at various heights by placing them on bricks, blocks, benches, tables and so on. Containers placed on boards with castors can be moved against a wall for protection from wind, hail and frost, or to follow the sun. They can also be moved indoors when fall frosts hit, thereby extending the growing season.

Air space may be used to good effect. Hanging pots and baskets may be attached to the underside of the balcony above, on pole hangers or wall brackets. Be sure to use only heavy duty brackets, fasteners, chains, wire and ropes.

Overwintering Effects
The beauty of a small garden does not have to end in the winter. Plant trees and shrubs with coloured bark, such as Yellowwood and dogwoods (with yellow and red bark). Evergreens, which keep their foliage through winter, may also be used to brighten up the

FLOWER GARDENING

Apart from trees and shrubs, all other garden plants, including the commonly grown garden flowers, are herbaceous.

HERBACEOUS PLANTS

Herbaceous plants develop non-permanent, non-woody shoots that die back to ground level at the end of each growing season. There are three classes: perennials, biennials and annuals.

Perennials live for three or more growing seasons. They overwinter as dormant, underground or near-ground-level bulbs, corms, tubers, tuberous roots, roots, bulbs and shootlet systems from which new shoots, foliage and flowers are produced each growing season.

From a cultural point of view there are two basic kinds:

Hardy which includes all herbaceous over-wintering, garden plants, usually called simply, "perennials," such as delphiniums, lupin, lily, peony and blanket flower.

Tender which won't survive the winter outdoors, including the old favourites, dahlia, gladiolus and tuberous begonia.

Biennials live for two growing seasons. During the first they grow from seed, forming a non-flowering rosette of foliage which overwinters. In the next growing season, they flower, set seed and die. Canterbury Bell, Foxglove and Sweet William are biennials (or are treated as such).

Annuals live one growing season, during which they grow from seed, flower, set seed and die. In addition to the true annuals, some tender perennials are treated by gardeners as annuals since they flower from seed in one season. Annuals include most of the popular bedding plants.

Although technically tender woody perennials, from a cultural point of view Geranium (Pelargonium) and Fuchsia are also treated as annuals.

Annuals, biennials and herbaceous perennials provide "flower power" from early spring until the snow flies.

48 · GARDENING IN TORONTO

LANDSCAPING

Architectural elements in an urban garden.

• The wrought-iron railing is in keeping with the architecture. Note the interesting weeping form of the variegated ornamental grass.

Textural contrasts.

Folige variety.

• The use of contrasting and harmonizing foliage forms add long-term interest and variety to a small, tranquil garden.

• A variety of foliage textures. In the background, a Mountain Ash is beginning to produce its masses of brilliant scarlet berries.

• The use of broken, crazy paving blocks add a strong informal element to this small urban front garden. This contrasts strongly with the rather austere formality of the evergreen topiary.

A striking pathway.

Paving texture.

• Evenly spaced paving blocks create an interesting, coarsely textured patio. The black, wrought-iron furniture adds a nice, contrasting touch. Note how the natural wood siding on the house forms an integral part of the garden's strong sense of enclosure and privacy. *(above)*

Large-flowered, Pom-pom Dahlia in a container.

• While not the traditional way of growing them, many of the larger-flowered, taller varieties of dahlia are quite at home when grown in 30-40 cm containers. (*left*)

• In this mode, they provide the welcome element of height where several containers are placed together. Additionally, since they are portable, they provide the creative gardener with opportunities to rearrange the landscape from time to time.

• Bear in mind that dahlias in pots, when well-established, require copious watering, especially during hot, dry periods.

Cosmos atrosanguineus — tender, tuberous-rooted perennial.

• Use various kinds of tender bulbous plants to supplement and add variety to annuals and other bedding plants.

• Dahlias and Gladiolus can provide welcome extra colour in late summer and early fall.

• Long-season, summer-flowering, low carpets of brilliant colour can be created with Multiflora Begonia varieties such as Flamboyant, Helen Harmes and Richard Galle.

Double-flowered, Tuberous Begonia Hybrid (Begonia x tuberhybrida).

• The large-flowering, tuberous begonias grow best in locations exposed to the morning sun, but shaded during the sunniest and warmest part of the day.

• The stiff, upright, sword shaped leaves of gladiolus provide a strong contrast to most hardy perennials.

Begonia — multiflora hybrids.

• Double flowered, hybrid Tuberous Begonias are excellent in 10-15 cm diameter pots and containers. Also try a few large-flowered dahlias in large pots. The tender, tuberous-rooted, perennial, Bloody Cosmos can also be treated as a tender annual. Raise it from seed, in a warm environment, early in the year, just like bedding dahlias. *(above and right)*

Double-flowered, tuberous Begonia Hybrid (Begonia tuberhybrida).

Upward facing Lily Hybrids and Bee Balm (Monarda didyma "Cambridge Scarlet").

• True lilies (Lilium species and varieties) are true queens among herbaceous perennials. They are available in a wide range of species, varieties and hybrids. The majority are easy to grow.

• By careful selection, it is possible to have lilies in flower in the garden from May to October.

Puschkinia scilloides — a dwarf, Spring Bulb.

• Many hardy bulbs flower early in the spring, long before most other plants begin their growth cycle. As a consequence, they are an important source of early colour.

• Be generous in your plantings. Most of the smaller bulbs look best when in groups of 2 to 3 dozen plants.

• Plant hardy bulbs in early fall, as soon as the bulbs are available in garden centres and department stores.

• Tulips are the most popular bulb flower. They are available in a wide range of kinds from dwarfs such as Tulipa tarda to the giant Darwins and Fosteriana varieties.

• Bear in mind that planting location will influence the flowering time of tulips. Bulbs in warm, south or southwest facing locations will flower up to six weeks earlier than the same variety in a semi-shaded, cooler place.

• Many dwarf kinds are well suited to sunny spots in the rock garden.

Crocus susianus — an early spring-flowering bulbous plant.

Autumn Crocus (Colchicum autumnale) — a fall-flowering bulb.

• Autumn Crocus provides a welcome touch of bright colour prior to the onset of winter.

• There are several species and varieties of Autumn Crocus or Colchicum. Most kinds produce their spectacular, crocus-like flowers in the autumn, before the foliage emerges, in stark, colourful contrast with surrounding bare soil.

• The foliage pokes through the soil in the following spring, dying down again in summer.

Tulips — Governor General's Residence, Toronto.

Love-lies-bleeding (Amananthus caudatus) — a tender annual.

Tree Mallow (Lavetera trimestris) — an annual.

• Excepting shrubs and trees with brightly coloured foliage, annuals provide the longest period of summer colour — from June to October, depending on the final, fall frost. No other group of herbaceous plants can compete in this arena.

Painted Tongue (Salpiglossis sinuata) — an annual.

• Don't forget that there are many hardy and half-hardy annuals that can be raised from seeds sown directly outside in the garden from mid April to mid May. The keys are sowing thinly and thinning out the resulting seedlings 15-30 cm apart depending on the height and spread of the particular plant.

• When purchasing annual bedding plants, select those that are: not crowded in their flats, short jointed — not long and lank, mid to deep green — not pale green or yellowish. There is no particular merit to plants being in flower, as long as they are of reasonable size.

Moss Rose — (Portulaca grandiflora cultivar).

Castor Bean (Ricinus communis "Impala") — young fruits and male flowers.

• For a truly sub-tropical effect, try Castor Bean Plant and the large-flowered Datura meteloides. Use greenhouse-raised, potted seedlings. (*above*)

CONTAINERS & TRELLISES

Hanging Basket — Ivy-leafed Pelargoniums (Common Geranium), petunias and the trailing Black-eyed Susan.

• Most annual flowers are very much at home in containers.

• Drought tolerant kinds such as Pelargoniums (Common and Ivy-leaved Geraniums, Petunias, Zinnias, African and French Marigolds, African Daisies and Dusty Miller are particularly well adapted.

Hanging container on high trellis — Zonal and Ivy-leaved Pelargoniums (Common Geraniums) and purple, trailing Lobelia (Lobelia erinus cultivar).

• Called the "queen" of climbing plants by many experienced gardeners, Jackman's Clematis and the related members of the Jackman group, deserve a place in every garden. *(left)*

• Keys to success in growing Clematis include a shaded root zone, head in the sun and plenty of water and fertilizer during the growing season.

Jackmans Clematis (Clematis x jackmanii) — a summer-flowering climber.

A white, small-flowered Clematis.

• Regular watering is a key to success, especially when the containers are full of well-ramified plant roots and the plants are approaching their peak of development. Check twice daily and water as soon as the soil surface begins to dry and turn lighter coloured. In hot dry weather — one or two waterings per day may be necessary.

Half-round, hanging baskets on an archway wall.

• Place hanging baskets against a background of foliage, stained siding or masonry. Avoid locations where other growing plants can obstruct them from view.

• In hanging baskets, consider both upright-bushy and trailing plants to provide contrast in forms.

• Low, brick-walled planters are excellent when planted with a single, strong coloured bedding plant such as dwarf impatiens and Multiflora Begonias.

An urban back garden   Arcadia Junipor, Marigold, Trellis with hanging baskets, Plastic Pots of Annuals, and Sumac in the background.

Wisley Gardens (R.H.S.) A demonstration garden with rustic trellis-work, and a raised bed of Red Impatiens.

Containers with Pelargoniums (Geraniums), snapdragons and marigolds.

• Close and open-work trellises are excellent architectural elements in the garden. They may be used to create screens, lath-houses, pillars, pergolas and archways.

BULBS, CORMS AND TUBERS

The term "bulb," as generally used by gardeners, includes many underground storage structures, including bulbs, corms, tubers, tuberous roots and rhizomes. All such bulbous plants are hardy or tender herbaceous perennials.

Bulbs • A true bulb is a compressed, telescoped shoot, with a flattish plate at its base, from which a more or less rounded to pear-shaped mass of fleshy leaves emerges above and roots below. Leaves are closely folded over one another and in some kinds (tunicated bulbs, such as tulips and onions) the leaves wrap around the bulb and the outer leaves are thin and papery. In others (scaly bulbs, such as lilies and fritillarias), the leaves simply overlap each other. The flowering shoot develops inside the bulb, emerging from the top at the appropriate time.

Corms • A corm is a compressed, telescoped thickened stem, enclosed by thin, papery leaves. Leaves and flower stems arise from buds at the top of the corm and roots emerge from the base. During the growing season the corm gradually shrivels, becoming flat and brown by the end of the year; a new corm develops on top of the old corm. Examples are crocus and gladiolus.

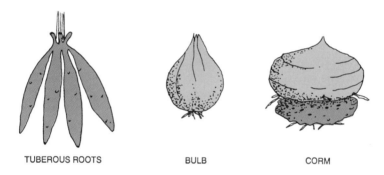

TUBEROUS ROOTS   BULB   CORM

Tuberous Root Systems • In a tuberous root system, one to several finger-thick or sausage-like fleshy roots are attached to the base of the vegetative and/or flowering shoot or shoots. Old shoots die back to ground level after flowering. New shoots arise from the buds at the base of the shoots of the previous season, rather than directly from the roots. This is of great importance since a tuberous root without a piece of old stem and at least one bud won't produce a plant. During the growing season the clump of roots increases in size. A dahlia has a tuberous root system.

Tubers • A tuber is a compressed, telescoped, thickened stem without any obvious leaves but with buds, such as in the potato. The shape may vary from rounded, flattened, dish-like (such as begonia), to formless and multinode (such as anemone). Vegetative and flowering shoots arise from buds on top of the tuber; roots emerge from the base. During the growing season the tuber increases in size. Caladium is another example of a tuber.

Rhizomes • A rhizome is a thickened stem that grows underground or along the soil surface with roots below and buds (eyes) above. The Bearded Iris is an example.

CULTIVATION

During the past decade, the use of perennials has increased immensely in the Metro Toronto area, because they can flower, grow and increase year after year. Many perennials are hardy, long lived, do not require regular division and thus can be used in bedding schemes and mixed borders to provide broad sweeps of colour, texture and contrast of a permanent nature.

By nature, perennials are deep-rooted. Perennial border preparation, care and culture differs from that required by annuals, since perennial beds are more deeply cultivated. However, many of our native perennials survive on shallow soils and are better suited to wildflower plantings.

Firstly eliminate perennial weeds, such as twitch grass and bindweed. Following weed control, cultivate as deeply as possible: to 45 cm. Break up any hard pan by deep digging to provide adequate drainage. Double digging, as explained in *Chapter 3*, is an ideal soil preparation for a new perennial border.

To improve soils, add large amounts of compost, well rotted manure or peat moss. Prior to planting, incorporate commercial fertilizer with a high phosphorous analysis, such as 5-20-10, at the rate of 0.5 to 1 kg per 10 m².

Choice of perennials will be determined by the garden's environment. Fortunately there are selections for any situation.

Prepare beds and borders in late summer, cultivate a few times to reduce annual weeds, and plant in early fall for best results. To avoid freeze-thaw problems and subsequent heaving and drying-out of fine rootlets, the beds should be mulched for the first winter. Leaves, wood chips or bark mulch are adequate. Perennials take more than one growing season to "fill in"; therefore, weed control is necessary. This includes traditional hoeing and mulches. Routine maintenance such as deadheading flowers, (trimming back after flowering to encourage another surge of bloom) and removal of dead foliage in either late fall or late spring may be necessary. Sometimes, the practice of leaving foliage during the winter will help to trap snow and provide winter cover.

THINNING

Thinning is the removal of young shoots from the crown of a plant, and it is done in order to stimulate the remaining shoots to grow taller, stronger and healthier and to produce larger flowers. Most herbaceous perennials that benefit from thinning have one or more of the following characteristics:

• they form large clumps of vigorous, closely spaced, sometimes invasive shoots;

• they produce several closely spaced, competing shoots, originating within a small area;

• they produce a large number of weak spindly shoots.

There is no need to thin plants that produce few, non-competing shoots from a small, indefinite, slow-growing crown.

Thinning should be carried out early in the growing season before new shoots are more than 8 cm long. Staking should be done at the same time. Thinning can be accomplished by using a thumb nail and twisting off the stem that needs to be thinned, or by using a sharp knife.

DIVIDING AND REPLANTING

Hardy, herbaceous perennials need to be lifted, divided and replanted periodically. For most varieties, this procedure is carried out every three to five years; however, the frequency varies.

Short-lived heavy feeders like Shasta Daisy may need replanting every one to two years. Lift lilies and hostas at 5 to 10 year intervals, peonies once every 10 to 20 years and tall bearded iris every three years. Some perennials with small, slow-growing crowns, producing shoots that never show reduced vigour and health, may seldom, if ever, need dividing. When worn out, these may simply be replaced with new plants.

Indicators that division is required include the following:

• Plants develop a large clump of closely spaced overcrowded shoots that spread beyond their allotted space;

• Several satellite, daughter plants from underground runners pop up away from the main clump;

• There is an obvious reduction in height;

• There is a deterioration in health, vigour and quality of shoot and foliage growth and a reduction in size, colour and quality of flowers.

Plants that may not need dividing include:

• Those with a single, or a few, closely spaced crowns, which have nothing to divide;

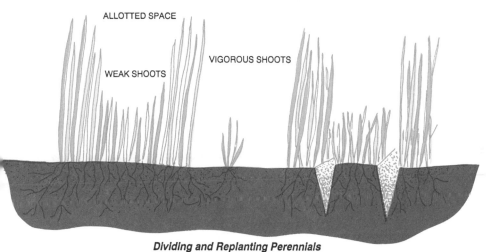

Dividing and Replanting Perennials

- Those with small clumps of crowns carrying small, evenly spaced buds, each producing a shoot of roughly equal size and vigour, where there is little or no difference in vigour between peripheral shoots and those originating in the centre of the clump or crown;
- Those with clumps that don't increase in size or increase very slowly;
- Those that have tap roots and small crowns, producing a few shoots within a small area of soil.

The general rule of thumb for timing of division is that spring-flowering plants are divided in the fall, and fall-flowering plants are divided in the spring. The few exceptions are plants that flower towards midsummer and can be easily divided after flowering. These include beardless and bearded iris, and primulas.

INSECTS AND DISEASES

Perennials are subject to much the same insects as annuals and vegetables, and should be closely observed and treated as required.

Leaf Blight • Diseases such as leaf blight may occur with antirrhinum, chrysanthemum, delphinium, lupins and peonies and primulas. Small to large spots of various colours may develop on leaves, and their centres may drop out to produce a shot-hole effect. These may be controlled by fungicide applications.

Mildew • Powdery mildew, a white powdery covering on stems and leaves, is common with delphinium, phlox, chrysanthemum and bluebells, and is more prevalent where the humidity is high and the nights are cool. Use resistant cultivars and plant in sunny locations with air circulation.

Leaf Hoppers • Blooms that are stunted, distorted and a greenish-yellow colour on asters, English Daisy and Black-eyed Susan are symptoms of ''yellows''. This disease is transmitted by the six-spotted leaf hopper. Although there is no control for the disease, controlling the leaf hoppers will help.

Slugs • Slugs are always a problem. They like campanula, delphinium, hosta, primula, viola and lilies. Slugs generally eat during cold, damp periods, feeding at night and leaving slimy trails. Treat with slug-baits.

Thrips • These have rasping mouth parts and produce silvering on leaves and distortion of blooms and leaves. Treat when observed. They can attack begonia, bluebell, gladiolus, day lily, iris and lilies.

GROWING PERENNIALS FROM SEED

Species, varieties and cultivars, that come true from seed are sown in a sterilized medium in mid-June to July and placed outdoors in light shade. Keep the medium moist until germination is complete, water early in the day and, if in cold frames, ventilate to avoid damping off. At the true-leaf stage, transplant into cell packs or 5 cm pots and then plant into open ground in the fall. If the plants are not large enough in the fall they can be overwintered in a cold frame under mulch, and planted out in beds the following spring.

A number of perennial seeds require a chilling period prior to germination. Sweet Woodruff, Gasplant, Fringed Gentian, alpines, and primulas require this treatment. For those cultivars and selections that do not come true from seed, such as double-flowered varieties, cuttings or division will be required.

PERENNIAL SELECTION

The selection of perennials for any given situation requires considerable knowledge of plant textures, growth habits, flower colour and period of bloom. In sunny locations, Creeping Cinquefoil may be combined with Bloody Cranesbill in the foreground. In shade, Plantain Lily and Sweet Woodruff provide excellent textural contrast.

Grey-foliaged plants are effective in separating colours. Perennials can be combined with a number of other plants such as annuals, biennials, flowering shrubs and spring-flowering bulbs. The bulbs are particularly easy to use since they bloom much earlier than their companion plants, and their foliage has died down when the perennials are in full bloom. Some combinations that may be successful include narcissus interplanted with low-growing ground cover such as Deadnettle, Sweet Woodruff or Creeping Cinquefoil.

Narcissi can also be used with perennials that leaf out later in the season, such as Plantain Lily or Black-eyed Susan. As the narcissi die down, foliage of the perennial takes over to reduce weed invasion. Early crocus can be planted with Mother-of-Thyme. Perennials such as Black-eyed Susan and Sedum Stonecrop are used to advantage with ornamental grasses.

Long used in Europe and the orient, grasses have been neglected as ornamentals throughout North America. Many species and cultivars native to our country are drought-tolerant and provide a long season of interest in the landscape, offering textural contrast during spring and attractive seed heads in fall and winter. They may be used as ground covers or as accents of upright form.

Natural landscapes and drifts of herbaceous perennials encourage an increase in wildlife populations, particularly birds and butterflies. Select plants that produce pollen, nectar or seed to attract wildlife. Among the species that encourage butterflies, are New York and New England Asters, the parents of the garden Michaelmas Daisy. Goldenrod attracts to Red Admirals, Monarchs and Painted Ladies.

The basic considerations for any planned perennial planting include:
- *combining early-, mid- and late-season perennials for a long season of bloom;*
- *gradation of height from compact types in the foreground to taller ones in the background;*
- *texture contrasts (the placement of coarse-leaved adjacent to fine-textured plants, for example);*
- *colour contrast and harmony.*

BIENNIALS

Biennials such as English Daisy, Sweet William, Forget-me-Not, Iceland Poppies and pansies can be used in mixed borders. They are generally seeded in early summer, much the same as perennials, and then transplanted into permanent positions in early fall or overwintered in cold frames, then planted out the following spring. Many biennials self-seed and if conditions are favourable will occupy permanent sites. Gloriosa Daisy, Sweet William, Iceland Poppy and Forget-me-Not can easily do this.

ANNUALS

Still the most extensively grown herbaceous plants, annuals may be purchased as bedding plants or grown from seed.

BEDDING PLANTS

Annuals can be obtained from a multitude of outlets in the spring: as soon as the threat of frost is over, greenhouses, garden centres and retail outlets all set up sales stations. This keeps prices competitive; however, the selection may not be very broad.

When selecting and purchasing annuals, look for compact, well branched sturdy plants with developing flower buds. Straggly, drawn-out shoots and foliage, and faded blooms indicate that plants have been held too long in the greenhouse and will be set back when placed in the open. Bedding plants such as florists' geraniums are grown in 10 to 15 cm pots. They should possess one or two developing flower trusses.

Seeded annuals are sold in open flats, trays or in cell packs. Today, one can purchase annuals directly seeded into plugs which are smaller than cell packs. They are generally not in flower at the time of sale, but are cheaper.

Do not buy and plant too early in the season since there is a fifty percent chance of frost after May 10th to the 15th in the Metro Toronto area. It is generally wise to wait until mid-May or later when purchasing large quantities of annuals.

ANNUALS FROM SEED

To save money, consider growing plants from seed. Annuals can be grown in sunny windowsills, under fluorescent lights, or in a glassed-in, frost free porch. There is tendency to sow seed too early; check the seed catalogues for the number of weeks from seeding to flowering and gauge your timing accordingly. Fibrous rooted begonias, for instance, should be seeded in January, while marigolds are not seeded until early April.

Soil is a key factor in good seed germination. It should retain moisture, be well aerated, be light and of a pH between 6 and 7. The home gardener is advised to purchase seed soil mixes which contain peat moss, vermiculite, perlite or turface in varying proportions. They are free of insects, diseases and weed seeds that can reduce seedling growth.

Seedling containers come in many shapes and sizes: egg cartons, plastic margarine tubs, foam cups, standard 15 to 20 cm clay pots and special plastic flats with individual compartments. These are particularly compact and also come with clear plastic tops, providing a greenhouse for germination. Another of their advantages is their capability to accommodate a different type of annual in each compartment.

Put the soil mixture into the flat and firm it well with your finger-tips. Tamp the soil with a flat piece of board, keeping the soil level at least 6 mm below the rim of the pot or flat, then place the container in a sink of water until it seeps up and darkens the surface of the soil. Allow it to drain. Broadcast (scatter) seed randomly over the soil surface if using pots. Where plastic or wooden flats are used, sow in drills. These are made by pressing the edge of the board into the soil to make parallel depressions, which are seeded and then covered lightly with fine soil. Very fine seeds such as those of the begonias are not covered.

Label each container or row with a standard label using a waterproof marker. Cover the seed pots with glass, plastic, or newspaper until germination occurs. Once seeds have germinated, water from below by soaking. Do this early in the day and allow the water to drain thoroughly to avoid "damping off" problems.

To avoid straggly, drawn out plants, thin out the seedlings as indicated in *Chapter 6* or "prick out" (transplant) into cell packs, peat pots, trays or plastic pots. The first leaves to appear after germination are cotyledons which supply food to the emerging seedling. Prick out when the first pair of true leaves appear above the cotyledons and the plant is sturdy enough to be moved.

To prick out, push under the roots of the seedlings with a knife blade and ease them up and out of the flat. Gently tease them apart. Make a hole in the soil with your finger or the knife blade, drop the seedling in place and lightly firm the soil around it with the fingers. Water thoroughly after pricking out and keep the seedlings in the shade for a few days to avoid excessive wilting. Feeding with a liquid fertilizer, high in phosphorous, can be done at this time. All watering and feeding should be done early in the day.

Pay attention to air circulation and ventilation to prevent soil-borne diseases which may cause collapse of the seedling at the stem. Fungicides can be applied as a drench to solve this problem. Fungus gnats, aphids and spider mites may affect seedling growth and should be controlled when observed. As seedlings grow they can be hardened off by lowering the temperature or moving them to a cooler frost-free location. Pinching out the growing tips may be required to produce bushier, more compact plants.

Whatever container is used, it should possess basal holes to facilitate drainage. Seeds require moisture to start germination and oxygen for root development. Temperature is a third essential factor: annual seeds need a minimum temperature of 10°C.

PLANTING OUTDOORS

Seeding annuals outdoors should not be left too late. As soon as the soil is workable and heavy frosts are over, annuals can be seeded in prepared beds, or broadcast where a naturalized appearance is required. In Toronto, sow by mid-May and thin out if seeds germinate too thickly.

Cosmos, African Daisy, California Poppy, Cornflower and Baby's Breath may be sown outside. Annual bed preparation is similar to that suggested for vegetables. Add organic matter and a complete fertilizer low in nitrogen, such as a 5-10-10, at the rate of 0.2 to 0.5 kg per 10 m² Rake the soil level and mark out areas for annual plantings. These may be formal beds, or informal drifts in mixed borders.

Annuals in flats, pots and other containers should be watered prior to transplanting. Dig a hole with a trowel, insert the plant, firm it in and water well. Water daily until annuals are established, then decrease the frequency as they grow. Keep weeds in check, feed with liquid fertilizer every 3 to 4 weeks, and remove faded flowers to encourage new blooms.

Mulches such as landscape fabric, black plastic and pine bark can be applied to annual plantings to reduce weeds, conserve moisture and moderate soil temperatures. Tall annuals may require staking and tying. Metal stakes that can be linked together are available.

Insects can also be a problem. Aphids attack many annuals and should be controlled when observed. Beetles, bugs and caterpillars that chew and damage the leaf, stem or flower should be treated when observed with a contact pesticide, or be hand picked. Leaf hoppers are common on delphinium, lupin, and zinnia. These are small, greenish insects that feed on the underside of the leaves and jump quickly when disturbed. They cause a stipple or scorch symptom to appear on the upper side of the leaves. Treat with a contact spray. Mites may attack antirrhinum, begonia, gladiolus, phlox and zinnia. Again, treat when observed but repeat treatment every 5 to 7 days over a 21 day period. Treat slugs and thrips as described in the perennial section.

Early fall frost, if light, may not cause too much damage to annuals. Those that are blackened should be removed; others may be left until bulb-planting time.

ANNUAL SELECTION

According to Bedding Plants Incorporated, the most favoured annuals grown in North America, in order of preference, are: impatiens, geraniums, petunias, marigolds and begonia. Gardeners should begin with these easy-to-grow varieties.

Impatiens • Intensive breeding programs have resulted in a number of very good varieties. These have red, pink, orange and red flowers, and do well in shade or partial shade. They prefer moist soils and should be adequately watered. Dry soils inhibit flowering and may cause flower drop. The Super Elfin and Princess series are popular. Sweet Sue, the first New Guinea impatiens grown from seed, is a stocky branching plant with 5 to 7 cm flaming orange blooms. It prefers partial sun.

Geraniums • These are perennial in tropical climates. Geraniums can be produced both from seed and cuttings and are favoured for use in planters and hanging baskets as well as in the garden. Their bright red, white or pink flowers contrast well with evergreen plantings.New seedling types such as the Sprinter series and improves cultivars raised from cuttings has increased their popularity. Sunny, well drained soils are required for geraniums.

Petunias • Used extensively in hot, dry, sunny locations, petunias are available in a wide range of colours and a variety of flower sizes, shapes and forms. For best results, place petunias in full sun in well drained soils.

Marigolds • The bright warm colours exhibited by marigolds have dramatically increased their popularity for annual bedding. The orange and yellow colours blend well with the reds and orange-reds of geraniums and salvias, and their fine leaf texture contrasts well with more coarsely leaved annuals. A plant which prefers well drained soils in full sun, the marigold competes with petunias for hardiness and continuity of bloom. The African marigold is generally taller, more vigorous and has larger flowers than the French marigold. The Jubilee series, which grows as high as 40 to 50 cm, is very popular. In the more finely foliaged and smaller-flowered French marigolds, the Petite series are exceptionally good.

BULBOUS PLANTS

HARDY BULBOUS PLANTS

Hardy bulbs are planted in the fall (Refer to *Chapter 3* for information on soil preparation). This group includes Glory-of-the-Snow, Trout Lily, Imperial Fritillaria, Snowdrop, Alpine Hyacinth, Bulbous Iris, Grape Hyacinth, daffodil, Striped Scilla, squill and tulip. It also includes crocus (a corm) and tuberous roots such as Windflower, Jack-in-the-Pulpit, Spring Beauty, Bleeding Heart, Winter Aconite, Desert Candle and Lily of the Valley. Beardless and Bearded Iris, and trilliums grow from rhizomes.

Spring- and summer-flowering hardy bulbs are planted as soon as beds are ready, prior to freeze-up in the fall. Generally the small bulbs are planted early, followed by daffodils and narcissi and finally tulips. Roots usually emerge after planting and prior to freeze-up.

Bulbs require a deep, well drained, fertile soil containing a moderate amount of organic matter. However, they will tolerate a wide range of soils including well drained, heavy clays. Decayed manure, compost or peat moss should be added to sandy soils prior to planting, but with heavier soils it is better to add these ingredients in late spring, prior to the planting of annuals. Organic matter may encourage bulb diseases and rotting, which are common on wet, poor-draining soils.

A complete fertilizer of a 9-9-6 analysis is an ideal bulb booster, providing better blooms with attractive larger leaves. Apply and rake the fertilizer in prior to planting at the rate of 0.5 to 1 kg per 10 m².

Carefully inspect bulbs for disease and insect damage. Store in a cool but frost-free area until planting time since excessive heat either in transit or in storage can damage bulbs, resulting in aborted flowers.

Plant bulbs at a uniform depth with a trowel. Special bulb planters and trowels with depth markings are available. Small formal beds may be excavated to planting depth, placing the soil on a plastic sheet. Set the bulbs on the base of the hole and cover with soil.

Planting depths vary for various types of bulbs. As a rule of thumb, bulbs should be planted at a depth twice the height of the bulb. Crocuses, which are very small bulbs, should be planted about 2.5 cm below the soil surface, while tulips which are much larger will be planted roughly about 15 cm down.

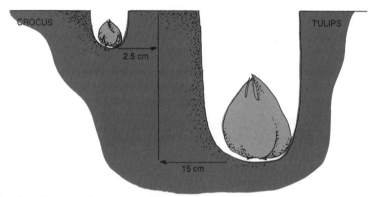

Planting distances between bulbs will vary according to growth habits, the final height of the plant in flower, and their purpose. Formal plantings with tulips, for example, may be spaced at 15 to 20 cm or more if inter-planted with low growing ground covers. Small bulbs such as scilla, Glory-of-the-Snow and crocus may be planted 5 to 7.5 cm apart. After bulbs are planted, rake the surface evenly.

FORMAL PLANTINGS

Formal beds are usually replanted annually with new bulbs. Good management and deeper planting may hold tulips for two or more years, although displays will be reduced after the first year. Where bulbs are left in place and inter-planted with annuals, remove flower heads and allow the foliage to mature and turn yellow. Cutting stems and foliage before maturation reduces its flowering ability in subsequent seasons. When foliage is withered and brown, gather and destroy it to prevent further diseases.

INFORMAL PLANTINGS

Natural plantings of narcissus and crocus will continue to multiply if left undisturbed. Dig and divide them only when they fail to bloom. Natural plantings — groups of bulbs — are usually made in lightly wooded areas, stream banks and rockeries. Narcissi, crocus, scillas, and muscari adapt well to naturalization where site and soil suit them. Large drifts of many bulbs are effective; scattering the bulbs over the ground and planting them where they fall produces a natural arrangement. When bulbs are naturalized in grass or under trees, a light feeding of complete fertilizer scattered over the surface of the ground, just as growth commences, will stimulate them and encourage vigorous growth. Again, foliage should be allowed to die naturally.

Scilla, Grape Hyacinth and Glory-of-the-Snow reproduce freely, so should not be planted in rockeries where they will crowd out more desirable plants. They are better planted around and under shrubs and in natural areas where they require little attention and can form an attractive spring carpet.

HARDY EARLY SPRING BULBS

Winter Aconites • These are the first bulbs to flower in the spring, often as the snow is just disappearing. They belong to the buttercup family and have yellow flowers. They self-seed and naturalize freely on sunny banks, under deciduous trees which provide summer shade. The tubers may appear dried, soak them overnight in water and then plant early in the fall, about 5 cm deep and 5 cm apart.

Crocus • Originating in the mountainous areas of Europe and Asia, crocuses bloom early. Colours range from white through yellows, oranges and blues, to lavender and purple. They are especially good for rock gardens, shrub borders and in great masses for naturalistic settings. Plant in mid-September. The larger types are the Dutch hybrids which have a range of bright colours. Other varieties, such as Cloth of Gold and Crocus-chrysanthus hybrids, in shades of blue, cream and yellow, flower earlier.

Glory-of-the-Snow • In its blue or pink forms, this flower is one of the earliest to bloom in the spring. Suited to the same locations as crocus, it is planted at the same time, 7.5 cm deep and 7.5 cm apart.

Grape Hyacinth (Muscari) • This thrives in naturalistic conditions and settings. It is also suitable for shrub borders and rock gardens where formality is not required. In open or naturalistic areas, the blue species, *Muscari botryoides*, will seed itself readily and so should be used where there is sufficient room for spreading.

Lebanon Squill or Puschkinia • These plants produce delicate, bell-like flowers of milky white or pale blue in loose clusters on 15 cm stems. They survive better in poorly drained soils than most bulbs. Plant 5 to 7.5 cm deep and 5 cm apart.

Blue Scilla • Not unlike the Glory-of-the-Snow in earliness, the scilla will often bloom before winter has really gone. The small, brilliant blue flowers are especially useful in rock gardens and naturalized areas. Scilla sibirica is a small species that is hardy and does equally well in sun and shade.

Snowdrops • This is one of the earliest spring-flowering bulbs. It prefers a well drained soil in partial shade. Nodding white flowers with green tips on slender stems appear as the snows melt.

Narcissus (including Daffodil) • Of the larger bulbs, the narcissus is one of the showiest. Both early spring-flowering species which are suitable for the front of borders and rockeries, and later-flowering, larger types that do well in mid-border locations and in naturalized situations, are available. Unlike tulips, narcissi produce new offsets from the central bulb each year, slowly increasing their share of the landscape. When flowering becomes sparse, clumps should be dug after bloom and replanted.

Classified for simplicity by the length of the trumpet in relation to the petals, or by species relationships, narcissi are available in large trumpets, small cups, doubles, and cultivars of recognizable species. The former provides such old favourites as King Alfred, a large trumpet yellow, and Mount Hood, a large trumpet white. Actaea, the true poet's narcissus, has a small red-tipped cup and white petals. Smaller, early trumpet types are provided by the cyclamineus group with reflexed petals. Jacksnipe and Tete-a-Tete are also reliable performers.

Tulips • Tulips are the most popular spring-flowering bulbs grown in Canada, outnumbering all other types combined. They are categorized below according to period of bloom.

Early • Single-early and double-early tulips flower in early May and come in brilliant colours. The doubles have heavier blooms and sometimes do not stand up as well as the singles. Included in this division are tulips related to *T. Kaufmannia, T. Fosteriana* and *T. Greigii*, and other tulip species. The former three have been hybridized with other types of tulips to produce short-stemmed, large flowered, brilliantly coloured early tulips. Kaufmannia, a very early tulip, has long red and white buds which open to reveal a creamy interior, usually marked at the base. In the Fosteriana group, Orange Emperor has striking apricot or orange flowers slightly larger than the others in its class. The Greigii tulips, named after the City of Toronto, are a vigorous-growing group with two or three red blooms per stem.

Mid-season • These tulips possess tall stems and the traditional tulip-glass shape of the Darwin flower. Apricot Beauty, with its soft rosy peach blooms, is an excellent Triumph tulip. The Darwin hybrid, Golden Appledorn, has deep golden blooms and conspicuous black centres.

Late-flowering • These tulips flower in early June. They include the Darwins, which are probably the most widely known tulips, producing flowers which are quite large, long, and strongly stemmed with a flat or square base. Olympic Flame is an example. The lily-flowered varieties, such as White Triumphator, possess graceful reflexed petals and brilliant colours.

There are also double late-flowering and single late-flowering tulips, The flowers of the double late look much like peony flowers, with their heavy blooms, and should be kept out of the wind. Of the single late tulips, Clara Butt, a brilliant rosy pink tulip, is favourite. Some of the most flamboyant late tulips belong to the Parrot group. These have deeply fringed petals and come in brilliant colours.

The names "narcissus" and "daffodil" are interchangeable. Narcissus is the generic name applied to this category of bulbs, and the name daffodil is simply a common name applied to the trumpet varieties. Of European, Asian and Northern African origin, daffodils are popular throughout the northern hemisphere.

One of the diseases that affects tulips is tulip fire (*Botrytis tulipae*). The leaves and flowers are affected with small brown spots and if the bulb is infected the plant is dwarfed and flowers stunted. At time of purchase, inspect bulbs carefully for bulb rot and tulip fire, and discard the affected bulbs. Bulbs may exhibit yellow or brown spots on the outer white scales with bulb rot, or may be covered with a pink, white or brown mold if infected with tulip fire. If you have this soil-borne disease do not plant bulbs in affected areas for four years.

HARDY SUMMER BULBOUS PLANTS

Hardy summer bulbs include irises, peonies and lilies. Generally taller than their spring-flowering counterparts, summer bulbs can be used in the middle of the border. They should not be planted over or near early spring bulbs, because their moisture requirement is greater at their period of flowering, when the early spring bulbs are ripening and do not require as much moisture. Some of the larger types, such as lilies, may require planting in the back of the border and must be staked, particularly on windy sites.

Flowering onions • Flowering onions are primarily summer-blooming, varying in height from golden garlic, with yellow blooms at 15 cm, to *Allium giganteum* species with its large purple spheres on 1.5 to 1.8 m stems. *Allium Christophi* is one of the finest of the flowering onions with large heads of starry lilac flowers in June. Plant alliums in fertile, well drained soils in sunny locations.

Irises • Many irises develop from rhizomes but there are also bulbous varieties. Bulbous irises should be planted early in the fall, and will bloom quite early in the spring. The *Iris reticulata* varieties Harmony and Cantab, with dark and pale blue flowers respectively, are ideal.

The rhizomatous iris varieties bloom in June with a variety of colours, making remarkable displays.

The bearded iris has marked beards on the lower petals or falls of the bloom. They are available in tall, intermediate and dwarf forms. Dwarf forms are ideal candidates for rock gardens, and flower earlier than the taller forms. Bearded iris prefer well drained, limey soils and are very tolerant of drought. Separate and replant the clumps every three or four years after flowering (July or August), and discard and burn any rhizomes affected by borers or disease.

The second group of rhizomatous iris, beardless iris, contain two outstanding members: Japanese and Siberian iris. Beards are lacking on the lower falls and the upper petals are smaller than the bearded types. These iris prefer moist, rich soil, and are better planted near pond and stream margins or in other wet areas, although Siberians will also do well in the ordinary border. Divide Japanese Iris either in early spring or late summer and Siberian Iris in late summer.

Peonies • The tuberous rooted peony is one of the most permanent perennial plants known to gardeners. It can thrive for 75 years in a single site. Its large showy flowers create beautiful displays in May and June and its foliage provides a backdrop for many other perennial plants in the garden.

Peonies should be planted in the fall, and spaced 1 to 1.5 m apart to accommodate their large spread. The soil should be well prepared before planting: good drainage is essential, with some manure or commercial fertilizer mixed into the soil. At planting time, add bone meal or a phosphate fertilizer to the soil for root establishment. Fall planting will help produce strong flower stems the following spring. Sunny locations are preferred but slight shade is tolerated; however, too much shade or planting too deep will reduce bloom power. When dividing and planting, be sure each division has at least three eyes, or buds, at the top of the tuberous root. Never plant the tuberous root with its eyes more than 5 cm below the soil surface. The plants require three years after transplanting to become fully established and bloom regularly.

Lilies • With better knowledge of their basic requirements, we can now use lilies in the garden much more than was possible in the past. The root stock is a true bulb whose scales overlap but do not envelop one another. The scales do not possess a protective covering, and can dry out. Therefore, they must not be exposed to drying air for any length of time. Freshly dug bulbs should be stored in moist peat moss or plastic bags and kept cool until replanted.

For best results, grow lilies in a sunny location, in borders with perennials, annuals, and low growing shrubs where root competition is minimal. Similar to other bulbous plants, lilies require well drained sites and prosper in raised beds or sloping areas. Deeply prepare the soil, since many of the lily bulbs are quite large and have to be planted at a depth of at least 15 cm. Some lilies produce roots from the bulb base and also from the stem above the bulb. These kinds should be planted deeply enough that stem roots can develop and help feed the growing plants. The Aurelian hybrids for instance, should be covered with 15 to 20 cm of soil, whereas smaller bulbs may only require 10 cm of soil cover. The Madonna Lily which shows very white, bright, tubular flowers in summer, is the exception since it produces its leaves from the bulbs in early September; it should be planted only 6 cm deep, to allow the basal leaves to reach the soil surface and function normally. Lily bulbs are best divided and replanted in the fall. Once planted they may be allowed to stay on-site for several years before division is required. In the outer areas of Metro Toronto, mulching may be required. General culture involves removal of faded blooms and seed heads and removal of dead stalks.

TENDER BULBOUS PLANTS (Summer and Fall)

Summer- and fall-flowering tender bulbs do not tolerate frost and must be dug and stored in a frost free location over winter. The most popular types are begonias, dahlias and gladiolus.

Begonias • Begonias are available in many types: upright growing, pendulous and multifloras. Upright types produce large blooms that may be rose-flowered, double, or with ruffled edges in many shades of pink, red, orange, white and yellow that contrast with the rich, dark green foliage. Pendulous types have smaller flowers and are used primarily in hanging baskets. Multifloras are more compact, bearing a multitude of small flowers, and can be used as a border-edging plant. Helen Harms is a yellow-flowering multiflora, Jewel of Ghent, salmon-copper and Queen Fabiola has coral pink flowers.

In the Metro Toronto area, place begonias where they receive no more than the early morning sun. Provide a rich soil well supplied with organic matter with good moisture-holding capacity. Fertilize regularly with a balanced liquid fertilizer to encourage large blooms and lush foliage. Although some begonias are tuberous others can be grown from seed, forming their tubers later in the season. Non-stop is a new variety grown from seed that provides numerous blooms with very bright yellow, orange, white, pink and red colours on small bedding-size plants.

Pot up tubers about mid-March, singly, in 10 to 15 cm pots depending on the tuber size. Make sure that the tubers will receive adequate light. Place the tuber in the pot so that the top portion of the tuber is barely above soil level. Keep indoors until the threat of frost is over; by June first they can be placed in the garden and watered frequently.

Dahlias • Initially dahlias can be treated the same way as begonias. However, they will tolerate more sunshine than begonias, and can be planted more deeply. Cover the growing bud or eye with 2.5 cm of soil.

Gladiolus • Gladiolus are lovers of sun, and prefer light sandy, well drained soils. They should be planted out in open soil when the native trees leaf out, since their tender spikes will not appear until a few weeks later when the danger of frost is over. A planting every two or three weeks will ensure a succession of summer bloom.

Colchicum • Often called Autumn Crocus, this is not a true crocus. Colchicum is planted in early August and exhibits large purple through lavender flowers from September to October, before the leaves emerge. *Colchicum autumnalis* and its varieties produce large bulbs that persist for many years. Since they develop coarse, strap-shaped leaves in early spring they should be planted among ground covers or in the middle ground of the border.

WINTER STORAGE OF TENDER BULBOUS PLANTS

In the fall after the first killing frost has blackened their foliage, dig up begonias and dahlias. Remove the soil from the tubers and allow them to dry in the sun for a few hours. Store them in flats, placed in a cool but frost-free storage area. Flats can be covered with peat moss to prevent their drying out. From time to time, check the bulbs for excessive drying or disease, culling and discarding affected bulbs.

Gladiolus corms are stored differently. Dig on a dry day, remove the stems and thoroughly dry the corms in the sun or under heat prior to storage. To control thrips, a real threat to gladiolus in Southern Ontario, dust all bulbs with an insecticide prior to storage, then store in flats with a wire mesh bottom which allows adequate air circulation and keeps the bulbs dry during the winter.

Planting annuals

SUNNY LOCATION

Annual Phlox
Baby's Breath
Cape Marigold
China Aster
Cockscomb
Common Heliotrope
Cornflower
Cosmos
Creeping Zinnia
Dusty Miller
Dwarf Verbena
Edging Lobelia
Flossflower
Flowering Tobacco
Geranium
Ice Plant
Joseph's Coat
Kochia
Lantana
Marigolds
Moss Rose
Nasturtium
Petunia
Pot Marigold
Scarlet Sage
Snapdragons
Spider Flower
Sunflower
Sweet Alyssum
Zinnias

PARTIAL SHADE LOCATION

Annual Candytuft
Annual Vinca
Browallia
Clarkia
Coleus
Cornflower
Cosmos
Dwarf Flossflower
Edging Lobelia
English Daisy
Flowering Tobacco
Forget-me-not
Pansy
Pinks
Pot Marigold
Purple Sage
Snapdragons
Spider Flower
Sweet Alyssum
Wax Begonia

HEAVY SHADE LOCATION

Annual Vinca
Browallia
Coleus
Edging Lobelia
Impatience
Pansy
Wax Begonia

CHAPTER 6

GROWING VEGETABLES

Today's vegetables have been improved in adaptability, yield, disease resistance and flavour due to plant breeding programs throughout Europe and North America. However, the pleasure of growing and picking fresh vegetables straight from the garden has not been supplanted by modern technology.

VEGETABLE GARDEN LOCATION

PLOT SIZE

Size of the plot will be influence by a number of factors such as the size of the family to be fed, the type of vegetables to be grown, availability of a suitable location and area, and perhaps the most critical factor; the amount of time available to cultivate and maintain the plot. Where space is limited the choice of vegetables will be important. For example, there is no need to plant vegetables that store well and can be purchased easily, such as potatoes. Vegetables like Brussels sprouts, that require a lot of room for planting, can be ruled out for gardens in smaller spaces.

A maximum yield can be obtained from a small plot with the method of successional sowing. For example, small quantities of lettuce are sown every two weeks so they do not mature all at once. Succession can go hand in hand with inter-cropping, where early lettuce is grown on a site later used for planting tomatoes. Much of this lettuce will mature prior to competing with the tomatoes.

See *Chapter 2* to help determine the location of your vegetable garden.

OPERATIONAL PLANNING

ORIENTATION OF ROWS

On relatively flat land, vegetable rows are oriented from north to south so that they receive the maximum daily sunlight. On a slope, plant along the contour of the land.

LOCATION OF VEGETABLES

Perennial vegetables such as asparagus and rhubarb are located at one end of the plot so that the area for annual plants can be easily cleared at season's end. Tall crops should be located on the northern end of the plot so that they do not cast

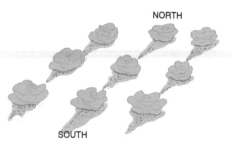

NORTH

SOUTH

Shade Tolerant Crops in North/South Rows

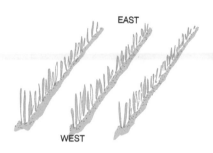

EAST

WEST

Sun-loving Plants in East/West Rows

Place Tall Plants on the North Side

shadows over other crops. Tomatoes and corn fall into this category. Tomatoes can also be located adjacent to fences or house walls using the vertical space instead of taking up an excessive amount of ground space. Stakes and trellises are other effective space savers to use when growing tomatoes, cucumbers and vining squash.

YIELD

My former garden exceeded 280 m², growing enough vegetables to supply fresh and frozen produce for a grown family of five. However, my neighbour of recent years built a raised bed of only 28 m² which supplied fresh vegetables to a family of four during the season, and a small surplus to neighbours. In my garden, an eight metre row of asparagus yielded 200 spears and 4.6 m rows of lima and bush beans supplied 4 L of each type. However, if you applied these figures to the neighbour's garden, yields could be doubled since row spacing can be much closer in raised beds, and therefore yield per unit area is greater.

CROP ROTATION

Throughout the Metro Toronto area, avoid planting vegetables under or near the roots of the black walnut tree. The roots exude a material called juglone which is toxic to most vegetables.

Crop rotation, an important control of insects and diseases, has been neglected in much of southern Ontario in favour of single or mono cropping with vegetables such as corn. The degradation and erosion of soil caused by this practice is just being recognized. Similarly, in your vegetable plot, continuous use of one location for one type of vegetable, for example, cole crops, may increase the incidence of diseases such as clubroot, a common cause of failure.

Many vegetables are closely related and subject to the same insect and disease problems. You may not be aware of the relationships since different parts of related vegetables are consumed. The potato and tomato, for instance, are both in the nightshade family. From the potato plant we use the tuber, but we use to fruit of the tomato plant. Basic vegetable families are:

- The *lily family*, including chives, garlic, onions and shallots
- The *mustard family*, including broccoli, Brussels sprouts, cabbage, cauliflower, Chinese cabbage, collards, kohlrabi, mustard, radishes, rutabaga and turnip
- The *gourd family*, including cucumber, gourds, melons, pumpkins, squash and watermelon
- The *parsley family*, which includes many of the herbs such as anise, caraway, chervil, coriander, cumin, dill, fennel, lovage, carrots, celeriac, celery, parsley and parsnip
- The *pea family*, containing broad, snap and lima beans, peanuts, peas and soybeans
- The *goosefoot family*: beets, spinach, Swiss chard
- The *nightshade family*: eggplant, peppers, potato and tomato.

METHODS OF CULTIVATION

ROWS

The common method of growing vegetables is on relatively level ground in the open garden. The distance between the rows is dictated by the means of cultivation; for example, a 50 cm roto-tiller will require rows to be set 70 cm apart. Because many row vegetables can be grown closer than this, the double row system is used to save space. Two rows of vegetables are grown approximately 15 to 20 cm or a hoe's width apart with each double row spaced the width of the cultivator apart. I grew most of my cool season crops, such as carrots, beets, beans and peas, this way. Close spacing may be used for hand-cultivated crops, perhaps 30-60 cm, depending on the specific crop. Crops that develop a large root system are generally planted individually in "stations": melons may be 1.8 m apart in single stations, and Brussels sprouts, 0.6 x 0.6 m apart

NARROW BEDS

Narrow beds are convenient where space is limited. Rows can be much closer together, always keeping the cultivating tools in mind when setting the row widths. It is much easier to run the hoe down a row of growing plants than to have to weed it by hand. A narrow gardening area allows one access to all parts of the bed from the sides.

As a rule of thumb, do not grow crops in the same family in the same location two years in a row. To help facilitate this method of crop rotation, during each growing season group family members close together. In this way, insect and disease problems can be controlled more easily.

RAISED BEDS

Raised beds are useful when the soil is poor. Clay soil, for example, dries more quickly and can be planted earlier when it is shaped into mounds using raised beds. This method of planting can also be helpful in areas with little topsoil, like Metro Toronto, where there is often less than 7 cm of topsoil on the ground.

To create raised beds, edge existing beds with treated lumber and fill with imported, screened topsoil. My neighbour grew a multitude of vegetables in such a bed. H e levelled part of his back yard and built a 9 x 3.5 m raised bed with 5 x 30 cm timbers; filled it, by bulk, with 8 parts topsoil, 2 parts vermiculite and 3 parts peat moss, rototilled this and then added 2 parts bagged sheep manure. Within this limited area he marked out nine sections, each 1 x 3 m, with 0.5 m wide paths between. He planted a variety of vegetables, one or two in each section, including Spanish and green onions, beets, beans, peas, carrots, kohlrabi, Swiss chard, snow peas, zucchini, radishes and lettuce, squash and tomatoes. It was very successful!

PREPARING THE GARDEN FOR PLANTING

Once you have decided which vegetables to grow, the next step is to prepare your garden and plant your crops. Refer to the section on "Kinds of Vegetables" and "Types of Crops" for help in deciding which vegetables to grow.

SOIL PREPARATION

Ideally, vegetable garden soil should be free of stones and debris, adequately drained and fertile. Most of the soils west, east and north of Toronto are heavy clay and require amending. See *Chapter 3* for general information about soil preparation. Organic matter such as compost, sterilized manure and green manure crops can be worked in to improve the soil texture and structure. I apply 90 to 200 kg of manure per 100 m^2, every other year. It can be ploughed in during the fall, leaving the soil in a rough state so that the freeze-thaw cycle of winter works the soil. When it is dry enough in the spring it can be roto-tilled before planting. A super-phosphate fertilizer, applied at 1 kg per 10 m^2 of soil area, promotes root growth. Additional nutrients may also be added depending on the crop. Although nutrients can always be supplied by standard fertilizers, it is my conviction that organic materials also improve the structure and texture of the soil the moisture holding capacity of soil, important in Toronto's hot dry summers.

SEED BED PREPARATION

In the spring, as soon as the soil is dry enough to support a rototiller or be spaded, an area for cool season crops should be prepared. Rototill or rough dig the soil, allow to dry for a few hours and then rake into a fine tilth, removing such debris as roots, stones and other trash. At this stage super-phosphate can be applied to the planting area. Raking debris is done with the teeth of the garden rake but smoothing and levelling for seed drills should be done with the back of the rake.

There are many ways to sow seeds successfully.

Two early crops, peas and fava beans, are large seeds and benefit from soaking overnight in water to swell the seed and initiate sprouting. A twine or string line stretched between two stakes is used to mark the rows. For larger seeds, a 2.5 cm deep drill is drawn with a draw hoe. The seeds are spaced evenly in the row; about 5 cm apart for peas and 7.5 cm for fava beans. Soil is drawn over the seeds and finally tamped (pressed) into place using the face of the rake. This ensures good soil-seed contact and eliminates air pockets which may cause drying out. Since these are sowned early, moisture levels are not a problem.

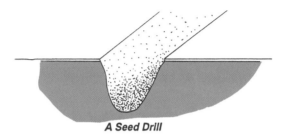

A Seed Drill

Fine seed such as carrots and lettuce are sown later in much shallower rows; the size of the seed indicates the depth at which it should be planted. Generally twice the diameter of the seed is sufficient. While peas and fava beans may be covered with 1 cm to 2.5 cm of soil and germinate easily, carrots and finer seeds need only about 3 mm to avoid suffocation. Some gardeners use vermiculite or sifted soil as a final cover for fine seeds. I use a proprietary seed sower in which fine vermiculite is mixed with the seed and sown at an aperture setting for thinner sowing resulting in less thinning out later. Always mark the end of the rows with a label indicating the type and variety of vegetable; many gardeners use the seed packet as an indicator.

SOWING IN WET SOIL

On wet soil, always work from a board or plank to minimize damage to soil texture. Using a pointed stick or the corner of a draw hoe, make a long narrow v-shaped seed drill in the soil surface at the correct depth for the vegetable being sown. Cover the drill with cloches or sheets of plastic for a few days prior to sowing, to warm and dry the soil; sow in the same manner as for dry soils. Alternatively, place dry peat moss in the bottom of the drill to soak up this moisture. Sow the seeds on top of the peat and cover with fine soil.

SOWING IN DRY SOIL AND DRY WEATHER

As described for wet or cold soils, draw a drill at the correct depth for the vegetable being sown. Thoroughly water the bottom of the drill using a watering can with a small diameter spout. Sow the seed and cover with dry soil to prevent evaporation.

FLUID SOWING

This method speeds up and controls sprouting, facilitates thin sowing, and promotes early growth and development.

Firstly pre-germinate the seed. Sprinkle it on moist blotting paper and place it in a temperature of about 21°C. As soon as the roots emerge from the seeds, mix them with a thick gel of dilute non-fungicidal wallpaper paste. Put the mixture in a plastic bag and cut off one corner. Slowly squeeze a stream out of the bag, laying it along the bottom of the seed drill and cover with soil.

OTHER SOWING METHODS

Other methods of seed sowing include station and broadcast methods. The station method is suitable for such things as cole crops, where three or four seeds are sown in the final location of each plant; after germination and when they have obtained their true leaves, they may be thinned out leaving one plant per station.

Broadcast sowing is tossing seeds randomly onto the ground where they will grow, after being lightly covered and watered in. Broadcast sowing is not for the novice. Inevitably weed and vegetable seeds germinate together. Row planting allows the garden to easily recognize seedlings, and to weed around them. There is no better control than running a hoe down between rows of seeds when the weeds are just showing. It is also easier to control damping off and insect and disease problems.

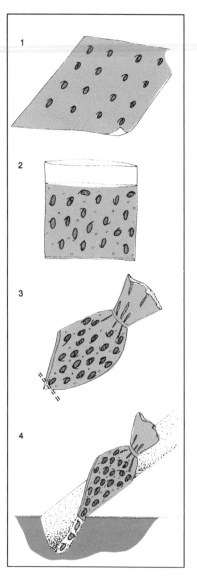

THINNING OUT

A major reason for poor crops of vegetables raised from seed is failing to thin out the seedlings or thinning them out too late. Some vegetables such as onions, scallions, radishes and bunching carrots are not thinned out but thinly sown and harvested when immature. Other vegetables, which are allowed to mature, need to be thinned to produce full size crops. As soon as the seedlings are large enough to handle, the surplus plants are removed, leaving the remaining seedlings spaced far enough apart that they have room to fully develop and mature.

Optimum production is achieved by thinning out in stages. For example, mature lettuce needs to be spaced 30 cm apart. First thin them to stand 7.5 cm apart. When the young plants touch, remove every alternate one, leaving the remaining plants 15 cm apart. Finally, again remove alternate plants, making room for those left to fully mature. This technique must be carried out with care.

Here are four practical pointers:

• Water the row of seedlings a day before thinning

• Nip off the seedlings using your nails rather than pulling them up

• Water the rows after thinning to settle the loose soil

• Disturb the remaining seedlings as little as possible

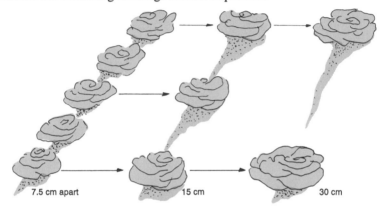

7.5 cm apart   15 cm   30 cm

Thinning Lettuce

TRANSPLANTING SEEDLINGS

Crops that require a long season of growth are often seeded indoors or grown commercially in a greenhouse. Seed is sown in rows or broadcast into flats or pots containing sterilized soil mix, then watered and covered until germination. Examples of crops seeded this way are Spanish onions, leeks, tomatoes and cole crops. Sown thinly or thinned out in the flats, the crops are grown for spring transplanting (For the seeding procedure, read about annuals in *Chapter 5*). Transplants raised outdoors are usually cool season crops that mature later in the season, such as Brussels sprouts, late cauliflower, broccoli and cabbage. They can be seeded in nursery beds as soon as the soil warms up.

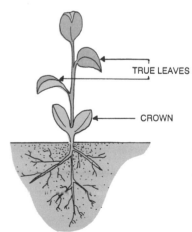

TRUE LEAVES

CROWN

Seedling Showing Its True Leaves

Growing on, or making your own seedlings for transplanting, is started with a seed bed relatively free of debris which possesses a fine tilth. Use a draw hoe to make rows, and sow the seed thinly. You may use a hand seeder, and mix the seed with fine sand and vermiculite. After sowing, cover the seeds with soil and tamp them with the back of the hows blade. When seedlings show their true leaves (the leaves that emerge after the seed leaves — see diagram), they may need thinning if the plants are very close together. Growing on, indoors or out, may require an application of liquid fertilizer. A starter type high in phosphorous encourages fibrous root systems and sturdy seedling transplants. Most of the cucurbits and lima beans, and certainly tomatoes, are best started indoors. Tomatoes require 5 to 8 weeks prior to transplanting and melons require as little as four weeks, so do not sow early.

BUYING TRANSPLANTS

Transplants may also be purchased from nurseries or garden centres. Most cucurbits and tomatoes will be in pots ready to set out in the garden. Look for healthy, dark green foliage. Avoid plants with thin, drawn out stems. Often the first truss of fruit may be evident or set. Watch for an excess of yellow, lower leaves or very dry soils in the pot. Cole crops are usually pulled with bare roots and bundled. Roots should be kept moist in wet paper, plastic or peat moss. Look for plants with turgid leaves that are not wilted.

With bare root transplants, keep the roots moist until planting time. If necessary, place the bundles in shallow trenches in a shady spot. Firm soil around the roots and water well. These can be held until conditions are suitable for planting.

SETTING OUT TRANSPLANTS

If possible, choose a dull, cloudy day for transplanting or if the weather is sunny, transplant in the evening to take advantage of the cooler temperature. Using strong twine and short stakes, lay out a line. Dig holes with a trowel, insert the plant and firm the soil around the roots with your hands or feet. Water in well. Watering may be required daily until the plants stand firm and are established. They will tend to wilt in the hot sun but if they stand up early in the morning they are doing fine.

Pot grown plants are tapped out of the pot, placed in a larger hole than for bare root plants, filled around by hand, firmed in, and watered well after planting. If transplants are dry, water them a few hours prior to planting. Transplanting pot-grown plants can be done any time since root disturbance is minimal.

KINDS OF VEGETABLES

Asking local gardeners is a good way to find out which vegetables may grow well in your garden. There are two minor categories of vegetables: cool season and warm season. Of these, some are shade-tolerant. Knowing which type your crops are will help you determine when and where to plant them.

COOL SEASON

Some of the more common, cool season garden vegetables are: asparagus; beets; broad beans (or fava beans); members of the mustard family including broccoli, Brussels sprouts, cabbage, Chinese cabbage, radishes, turnips and cauliflower; garlic; leek; onion; lettuce; members of the parsley family such as parsley, parsnip, carrots, celery and celeriac; kohlrabi; rutabaga; peas; potato; spinach; and Swiss chard.

WARM SEASON

Grown primarily for fruits and seeds, these require a long, warm, growing season to produce mature crops. Except corn, pole or runner, lima and bush beans, they are usually sown indoors, grown in pots and transplanted to the garden when danger of frost is past. Hot caps, plastic mulch and late season protection with cloches and other season extending covers may enhance growth and increase yields. This group includes eggplant, peppers, squash, tomato, cucumber, okra and melons.

SHADE TOLERANT

While most vegetables, particularly warm season kinds, grow best in reasonably sunny locations, a few will tolerate a semi-shaded spot or an area shaded during the heat of the day. These include: peas, carrots, bunching onions, lettuce, spinach and Chinese cabbage. Others that are worth trying in just a little shade are endive, kale, mustard greens, radish, Swiss chard, chives, mint and parsley. Such locations must be away from the roots of trees and have good soils.

WHEN TO START PLANTING

PLANTING COOL SEASON VEGETABLES

The novice gardener is often unsure when to plant cool season crops. Many believe that one must start planting on the first long weekend in May when, in fact, many cool season crops can withstand late spring frost and may be planted as soon as the soil is workable. The earliest sown are the frost-hardy types such as peas and broad or fava beans, which I have planted as early as the end of March. Much will depend on soil type and climate. Downtown Toronto locations that are near the lake, and have sandy soil, may be worked up to three weeks earlier than the heavy clays on the northern fringe of Metro.

SEMI-FROST HARDY

These group of vegetables, the semi-frost hardy types, are seeded early but will not germinate until soil temperature rises. The semi-frost hardy types, such as carrots, beets and lettuce, can be sown by early May. These will germinate later, when the soil temperature rises. The warm season or frost tender crops (e.g. tomatoes, bell peppers, eggplant, cucumber, squash) are delayed until the danger of frost is over, close to the first of June in the Metro area.

SOWING EARLY

There are several advantages to sowing cool season vegetables early. They mature best during the cooler weather, providing more than one picking before they dry on the vine. The harvest period for these crops is extended, which is particularly convenient for those who wish to store them frozen. Some other vegetables, such as Spanish onion, require a long growing season to mature and can be seeded inside cold frames, to be transplanted outside when conditions are favourable. Lettuce, leeks and spring cauliflower can also be started this way. A cold frame is an unheated, low, mini-greenhouse-like structure comprising wooden, concrete block or brick front, sides and back and a removable glass or plastic top. It may be a knock-down, winter-storable or permanent structure.

TYPES OF CROPS

POTATOES

Potatoes are planted in drills, two to three feet apart with 30 cm between plants in each drill. They may be seeded as whole seed or portions, as long as each piece has eyes or buds. Downtown, potatoes may be planted from mid-April to mid-May; in the suburbs, they may be planted later. Early potatoes are planted in mid-April, prior to the last frost in spring, and take two or three weeks to come through the soil. If frost does threaten, soil can be drawn over the new shoots to protect them. Prior to planting, a fertilizer high in phosphorous and potassium such as 5-20-10, at a rate of 7-9 kg per 100 m², should be worked into the soil.

Early potatoes such as Rideau are best for the homeowner since they are generally harvested before blight disease sets in and kills the stalks. Watch for the Colorado potato beetle, a foliage eater identified by its 2.5 cm length and black and yellow stripes. Hand pick and destroy these insects or use a contact pesticide as mentioned in *Chapter 10*.

ASPARAGUS

Asparagus is a perennial vegetable that requires fertile, deep dug soil. As with all perennial plantings, weed control can be a problem, so weeds should be cleaned out from the area long before plantig. Asparagus is the first vegetable of the season to be picked and should be planted in a sunny, protected site. Plants are placed 30 cm apart in rows one metre apart. Once the spears are harvested, filmy fronds appear. These are the permanent shoots and should be allowed to grow so that roots and crowns will develop for the following year.

COLE CROPS

Cole crops are cool season crops, grown for their edible foliage. Technically most are biennial, flowering in their second year; however, the edible vegetative portions are generally harvested in the first year and the plants are discarded before they are able to flower. They are raised from seed, sown indoors, and planted out early to produce early crops such as early cauliflower and spring cabbage. Cole crops can also be planted later in the season for fall harvesting. Brussels sprouts, broccoli, late cauliflower, Chinese cabbage, kale, kohlrabi, rutabaga and main-crop turnips are in this group.

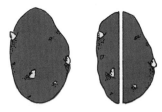

Dividing a Seed Potato

Early cabbage and cauliflower • These can be grown in rows 60 cm apart, with plants in each row 60 cm from each other. They can be transplanted by mid-April and harvested seventy days later. Both require fertile soils and moderate applications of nitrogen. Cauliflower leaves are tied over developing heads prior to maturity to prevent discolouration by the hot sun.

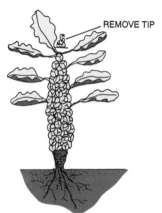

REMOVE TIP

White Rock cauliflower and Premium Crop broccoli • These brands can be transplanted by mid-June. They mature later and must be kept growing evenly during the summer months. Water the plants when they require it.

Brussels sprouts • Brussels sprouts, such as the Jade Cross types, require the greatest space and heaviest watering. Space them one metre by one metre apart. Nip out the growing points (shoot tips) when small, deep green buttons form where the leaves adjoin the main stem. This procedure produces larger sprouts that are easier to snap

Brussels Sprouts

off. Sprouts are sweeter if harvested after frost in the fall.

Pests of Cole Crops • The green caterpillar of the cabbage white butterfly causes considerable damage to cole crops. Control, when observed, by hand picking or with the biological insecticide Dipel.

LEAFY CROPS

Leafy crops, primarily used for salads, include leaf and head lettuce, Swiss chard, spinach and endive. Most are cool season crops, to be sown early, from April 1st to May 1st, or sown later to mature in early fall when the weather is cooler. Head lettuce is best sown in the cooler season. Sow rows 15 cm apart and thin to 5 cm between plants to produce good heads. The seed is very fine and should not be sown deeper than 6 mm.

BULB CROPS

Bulb Crops include Spanish onions, leeks, spring onions, onions from sets, shallots and chives. Sets are immature bulblets stored from the previous year's crop, to be planted by early April. They are harvested as early bulbs or green onions. Shallots are also grown from sets and are used for pickling. White sweet Spanish varieties form large bulbs. A popular brand of bunching onions is White Lisbon.

TOMATOES

This popular, warm season crop takes 62 to 82 days to mature after being transplanted into the garden. Tomatoes require a fertile soil, containing organic matter and a complete fertilizer low in nitrogen and high in phosphorous and potassium. Sturdy plants may be selected and set out when the danger of frost is over — May 10th in downtown Toronto, and May 15th in the suburbs. There is a 50% chance that a freeze will occur after these dates so keep hot caps or some form of protective covering available to put over the plants if frost is forecast. Generally, in the Toronto area, five clusters of fruit on each plant will develop and ripen during the harvest season. Each cluster, depending on the variety, yields 500 to 750 g of tomatoes, and each plant will yield between 2.2 and 3.2 kg. The larger un-staked types such as Bush Beefsteak require 90 cm between rows and plants; spacing for staked tomatoes can be reduced to 60 x 60 cm. Tomatoes benefit from black plastic mulches which reduce weeds and warm the soil in early summer.

Cherry tomatoes are popular for salads and can be grown in pots and planters. Sweet One Hundred is a good variety.

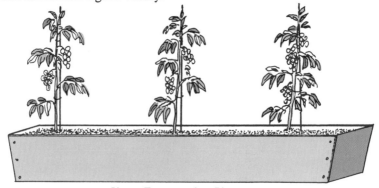

Cherry Tomatoes in a Planter

EGGPLANTS AND PEPPERS

The cultivation of these plants is similar to tomatoes. Space about 60 cm between rows and 30 cm between plants.

CUCURBITS

Cucurbits require rich, fertile soil and room to spread. Start indoors and transplant outdoors when the danger of frost is over. Cucumbers, muskmelons and cantaloupes require about 30 cm between plants and 1.5 m between rows. Pumpkins and watermelons require more space and moisture during the hot, dry summer season.

CORN

Corn such as Supersweet is seeded in open ground by early May, generally in double rows or in blocks to ensure that pollination by wind occurs.

ROOT VEGETABLES

Root vegetables include carrots, parsnip, salsify and beets. Generally sown by May 1st in drills 15 cm apart, they may be thinned out to between 5 to 10 cm apart. Parsnips should be thinned to 10 cm since they require a long season to mature. In the Toronto area they can overwinter outdoors and dug in early spring.

HARDY PEAS AND BEANS

Green peas and fava or broad beans can be sown as soon as the soil is workable prior to mid-May in Toronto. Plant in rows 30 to 60 cm apart with 2.5 to 5 cm between plants. Fava beans should have their tops pinched out when a few side pools have developed. This encourages an earlier crop and discourages black aphid which is the scourge of this plant. Lincoln, an old variety of pea, is a good one to start with. Little Marvel is smaller, requiring less room. Green, snap and pole beans are seeded later, when the warm season arrives, usually between May 5th and 25th, in rows spaced the same as those for peas and fava beans. Limas are often seeded indoors and transplanted by the third week in May to give them a long season of development. Pole beans, also called Scarlet Runners, are best when allowed to climb up poles, fences or trellises.

Support for Peas

PERENNIAL HERBS

Perennial herbs are best grown in perennial borders or in special formal garden areas close to the kitchen. Perennials such as chives, mint and thyme are easily grown. Mint can be very invasive, and should be put into a metal bucket with holes punched in the base to restrict it to a particular area. Tender herbs are grown from seed. Dill and cress, for example, are seeded in rows 60 cm apart, covered with 6 mm of soil, and thinned to 7.5 cm between plants. Summer savory, sage and thyme are sown the same way, but barely covered.

CHAPTER 7

FRUIT GROWING

A FRUIT GARDEN

Gardeners in Toronto can grow most of the tender fruits grown in more favourable locations, such as the Niagara Peninsula, where soil and shelters permit. Those in metro areas further north, east and west of Toronto are on colder clay soils, and may have to be satisfied with growing hardier fruits such as apples, pears and plums.

Unfortunately, fruit growing requires space, particularly when growing tree fruits. Where space is limited there are methods of pruning which can restrict growth to the vertical planes of walls and fences. Many fruit trees can be incorporated into the garden design, for instance, instead of planting ornamental crabapples, culinary varieties such as McIntosh and Idared can be used, thereby serving utilitarian and ornamental purposes.

Shrub fruits such as gooseberries, and black, red and white currants, can be used as informal hedges to create divisions or enclosures for your garden. Elderberries and hazelnuts can be used as large ornamental shrubs. Grape vines can be grown on fences, as dividers, or as a shade and fruit source on arbours, patios and decks. Strawberries can be grown as ground covers or as everbearers in barrels and planters.

TYPES OF FRUIT

From a horticultural point of view, there are basically five categories of fruits:

- Pome fruits usually contain several small seeds at the centre or core of a solid, fleshy fruit such as apples and pears.
- Stone fruits usually contain a large single stone seed in a soft, fleshy fruit, including plums, damsons, cherries, peaches, apricots and nectarines.
- Bush fruits usually contain several seeds in soft, pulpy, berry-like fruits borne in clusters. They include black, white and red currants, gooseberries and elderberries.
- Soft fruits is a category used for many seeded, soft, delicate fruits including strawberries, raspberries, blackberries, loganberries, etc., although several of these are also called bramble fruits.
- Vine fruits are varied, growing as climbing or trailing plants such as grapes and kiwi fruits.

LAYOUT AND SPACING

All fruit plants require sun for suitable ripening and should be located away from the shadow of large trees. Since they bloom relatively early, they require sites that are not subject to late spring frost.

Tree fruits can take up as much space as 9 x 12 m per tree for standards to 5.5 x 6 m for smaller cherries and pears to 3 x 3 m for dwarf apples. Apples and pears when grown as cordons (single double or triple upright stems), or with horizontal branches (espaliered) on the vertical plane of a wall, require less lateral space.

Bush fruits, such as currants and gooseberries, are oriented north-south in rows for optimum sunshine. Space them 1.2 m to 1.5 m apart, in rows 1.8 m to 3 m apart. Taller shrubs such as elderberries or raspberries require 3 m between plants and 3.5 m to 4.5 m between rows. Blackberries are brambles, and can spread a considerable distance during the growing season. They need to be 0.75 m to 0.9 m apart, with 1.8 m to 2.5 m of space between rows.

Vine fruits like grapes require 1.8 m to 2.5 m between plants. Strawberries, a ground covering fruit, require the least amount of space: they are grown 0.6 m apart, in rows 0.9 m to 1.2 m apart.

POLLINATION

Tree Fruits • At least two varieties of tree fruits must be grown together for successful pollination. Cross pollination occurs when eggs or ova in the female reproductive organs of the flowers are fertilized by pollen from the male reproductive organs or anthers of a different variety or cultivar of the same or similar type of fruit. In addition, they must be compatible: they must bloom at the same time. You may simply buy a variety compatible with your neighbour's tree, or you can plant two varieties. An example of a compatible combination of apple trees is McIntosh and Spartan.

Other Fruits • Fortunately, bush, ground cover and grapes are self fruitful and do not require other varieties for pollination.

SOIL CONDITIONS

Modern urban and suburban home sites seldom allow varying soil conditions. Fruit trees fortunately do well on a wide range of soil types as long as the soils are adequately drained. Apricots, cherries and peaches prefer sandy loam soils and are the most sensitive to poor drainage. Apples, pears, plums and grapes produce well on either sand or clay loams. Gooseberries and currants are best in a cool, well drained clay loam. On sandy soils, mulch to conserve moisture and adequate water during the growing season will be necessary. Open sites will also reduce mildew problems. Deep, well drained soils suit red, black and purple raspberries. Good air drainage and lots of sun are necessary for prolific crops.

> *Water Table*
> *Sites where the natural water table (the underground water level) is less than 90 cm down are not suitable for tree and bush fruits.*

TREE FRUITS

Usually, tree fruits are purchased as bare root or container-grown plants, for spring planting. The former type is cheaper but requires more care prior to planting. Buy from a reputable nurseryman and be sure that the type you purchase is grafted on the appropriate root stock. Choose well grown one or two year old trees, and watch for broken branches, dried out twigs and less than healthy buds.

MULTIPLE GRAFTED TREES

Nurserymen sell multiple grafted apple or pear trees, each tree carrying 4 to 5 different varieties. These so-called five-in-one trees have the advantages of ensuring cross pollination and providing a sequence of ripening fruits. A popular combination for apple trees includes McIntosh, Delicious, Northern Spy, Yellow Transparent and Tydeman Red. Particular care must be taken to control the more vigorous varieties in the combination. Northern Spy, for instance, grows faster than the other varieties and may sap the growth of its companions. Its side shoots must be summer pruned back to about four leaves beyond their point of origin.

BUYING OTHER FRUITS

Shrub, vine and ground cover fruits are also purchased and planted in the spring, mostly as bare root specimens. The same precautions used for bare root trees are required for these plants to ensure successful establishment.

Most of these bare root specimens come in plastic bags which, if kept closed, can be stored in the refrigerator until planting time. When planting, do not leave the plastic bagged plants in the sunshine — they may heat up and die. Bare root plants may appear dry at time of purchase. If so, soak the roots in water for 2 to 3 hours before planting.

CARE AND PLANTING

Tree and shrub planting are covered in *Chapter 8*; however there are some procedures specific to fruit trees and shrubs which are covered here.

Tree Fruits • For tree fruits, fertilizer may be required to encourage balanced growth, but not until the tree is well established, which may take two or three years. In general, fertilizer and water from lawn operations will aid tree growth. Too much nitrogen encourages vegetative growth at the expense of fruit and should be carefully controlled.

Bush Fruits • Some bush fruits, such as red raspberries, can be grown on wire supports stretched taut between posts at 4.5 to 6 m intervals. Control weeds by shallow hoeing and/or mulch with straw or pine bark. Feed each spring with approximately 175 to 225 g of 10-10-10 fertilizer per mature bush: spread the fertilizer under the branches and 30 cm beyond and work it into the soil. Water during the growing season and after harvest until late August particularly during droughts.

Support for Raspberries

Vine Fruits • Grapes are planted in a hole wide and deep enough to accommodate the root system. Do not put fertilizer or manure over the roots. Cover with topsoil, tramp well and water. Plant 2 to 3 m apart and, as growth proceeds, install horizontal trellis wires at 0.75, 1.25 and 1.75 m above soil level.

At planting time, remove all canes except the strongest. Twist this around the support string and tie into place; this will form the main stem. In the following year, when it has reached the top support wire. Next season, remove all shoots that develop below the bottom vine. Select six canes for future training. Prune them back each spring to 30-60 buds per plant (5-10 buds per stem.)

Ground Cover Fruits • Strawberries are planted early in the spring. Varieties that produce early runners yield more fruit than those forming runners later in the season.

The matted row system works best for strawberries. Set each plant so that the base of its crown is level with the ground surface, 0.6 m apart, in rows 0.9 - 1.2 m apart. Dig a hole deep enough to take the roots straight down and spreading out. Cover the roots with good topsoil, firm and water thoroughly. Allow runners to develop and produce new plants within the rows, but cultivate between the rows. Everbearing strawberries, which do not produce as many runners, may be grown on the hill system where plants are set 25 cm apart with 76 cm between rows. During the first few weeks after plants are set out, remove all the blossoms to encourage good establishment and runner production. After harvest, all runners are removed since these types produce fruit throughout the season. Mulching reduces weeds and conserves moisture. Plastic mulches and landscape fabric can be used effectively for everbearing strawberries.

PRUNING

POME FRUITS

Pome fruits like apples and pears can be grown in a number of forms for the home garden such as standard, half standard and bush, as defined in *Chapter 8*. The bush type is also available in smaller forms which are ideal where space is limited. Dwarf tree forms, their growth influenced by the root stock they are grown on, are often easier to spray for insect and disease problems than full-sized trees. Also, they can be pruned and harvest from the ground.

Dwarf Trees • The Malling rootstocks, M27, M9 and M26, produce dwarf trees approximately 15%, 25% and 40% of a full standard size, respectively. Dwarf trees should always be planted so that the swollen area on the trunk is above the final soil level. This is to prevent the grafted portion of the tree from rooting. If it roots from the scion, it will grow to normal size.

Blossom Removal and Thinning • For two or three years after planting, fruit trees should have their blossoms removed to encourage vegetative growth. Many standard trees do not fruit much until they are older, however dwarf types can fruit in the first and second years. The third year crop of fruit should be thinned, leaving a few to mature. Thereafter, some thinning may be required to encourage production of larger fruit.

Fruit Drop • When tree fruits reach a certain size, fruit drop may become a problem. This is a natural process, particularly during hot dry conditions, which allows only some of the fruit to mature. Watering during drought spells is a must if good crops are to develop.

Form Pruning • Cutting branches back indiscriminately does not reduce growth but encourages suckering and vegetative growth to the detriment of fruit production. Firstly, the newly planted tree has to be trained into a productive form, the simplest being the modified central leader which also produces a desirable shape for lawn trees. This trains and directs the growth into a permanent branch structure. The central stem of the tree (leader) and the lateral branches (scaffold limbs) form the primary structure. Scaffold limbs should be attached to the main trunk by wide angle crotches and be spaced at regular intervals around it. Until it starts to bear fruit for harvest, shape the tree by pruning very lightly. Prevent narrow angle crotches with branches that form an angle, less than 45° to the main trunk. Also remove dead or broken branches, surplus, competing leaders and branches that tend to grow towards the interior of the tree. As the tree matures, the pruning program should emphasize canopy development, aiming at a roughly pyramidal shape to maintain an open canopy where the fruit receives maximum sunlight.

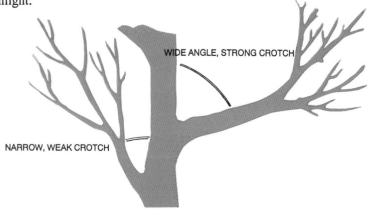

Different Branch Angles

How To Prune • Pruning cuts can be divided into two general procedures: heading back and thinning out.

Heading back involves shortening a leader branch or shoot to just above a bud or side branch to induce a significant increase in shoot growth from buds and side branches below the cut.

Thinning out is the complete removal of an entire competing leader side branch or shoot at its junction with a larger branch. It has a minor effect on subsequent vegetative growth.

For instance, heading back the central leader each spring by one quarter or one third of its length forces vigorous growth of several more or less upright shoots from buds below the cut and stimulates lower lateral branches to form wider crotch angles. When these upright new leaders are 10 to 15 cm long, select one to continue the central leader formation. This process should be discontinued when the tree has reached its final, intended height, at which time the leader is cut back to a lateral or side-branch at the desired height above ground. Pruning is confined to the dormant period just prior to active growth. On mature trees, excessively vigorous shoots (water sprouts) and shaded, weaker downward pointing shoots are removed.

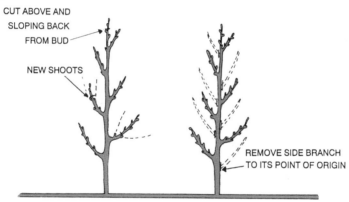

CUT ABOVE AND
SLOPING BACK
FROM BUD

NEW SHOOTS

REMOVE SIDE BRANCH
TO ITS POINT OF ORIGIN

Heading Back and Thinning Out

Summer Pruning • Summer pruning, to remove or reduce entire or portions of actively growing branches, thereby reducing tree vigour, may be needed to control excessively vigorous growth and improve fruit colour in heavily shaded canopies. Summer cuts should be limited to the removal of the current season's growth after the terminal buds (those at the tips of shoots), have formed and shoot growth has ceased, usually in late July to mid-August.

PRUNING STONE FRUITS

Stone fruits such as cherries, plums, peaches and nectarines are treated differently than apples and pears. First, since they are more subject to winter injury, they are pruned at specific times to minimize dieback and diseases such as peach canker.

Peaches and Nectarines • Peach canker disease can reduce the life span of these trees to 10 or 15 years. The severity of this disease is directly related to pruning practices. Peach and nectarine should be pruned when in bloom to identify the survival of dormant flower buds. Use the modified leader system for initial training. Peaches also lend themselves to fan or palm-shaped forms, enabling gardeners to take advantage of warm walls.

Cherries and Plums • At planting time, cherries and plums are headed back only slightly to a healthy bud and all lateral branches are removed. In July when new lateral shoots have formed, force them to form a 90° angle with the main stem using a clothes pin or tie them down to pegs fixed in the ground. The second year, remove all but four of these wide angled branches. These four remaining branches should be spaced equally in a spiral arrangement around the tree trunk, at least 13 cm apart vertically and laterally. The third year, select two to four more laterals to form a second tier of branches above the existing laterals. Remove excess side branches and any upright branches competing with the designated leader. By the fourth year the tree should possess six to eight scaffold limbs with wide angled crotches. Then remove excess limbs that are preventing light from reaching the lower parts of the tree.

BUSH FRUITS

Remove blossoms of bush fruits during the first year to aid establishment.

Black Currants • Retain 10 to 12 shoots, about one half of them one year old, and remove to 2.5 cm above ground level all those which are more than three years old.

Raspberries • Remove fruited canes to ground level after harvesting and reduce the number of remaining one year old shoots to 4 or 5 per plant by removing weaker suckers.

VINE FRUITS

During the first season of growth remove all shoots below the bottom wire that are not needed for lateral arms. Each spring select 6 canes from those of the previous year's growth for tying along the wires. Remove all other wood except one or two true bud spurs at each wire. Depending on vigour, 30 to 60 buds per vine will produce a crop after the third season. The fan system of training is preferable for vine fruits being grown in the outer areas of Metro Toronto. The trunk is kept below the bottom wire with two short arms, and canes are trained vertically from the arms in a fan shaped pattern.

WINTER PROTECTION

TREE FRUITS

The hardy tree fruits such as apples, pears, Montmorency cherries and plums do well in most locations in the Metro area, however, tender types require considerable protection from the cold northwest, winter winds. Peaches, apricots, sweet cherries and nectarines belong to this group and are easier to grow in downtown locations nearer to the moderating influence of Lake Ontario. Trees will be less susceptible to winter damage if fertilizer and water applications are reduced in the fall. This will encourage ripening of the wood by slowing down the tree's growth.

TREE AND BUSH FRUITS

Snow and ice can be a problem, breaking weak branches of fruit trees and bushes. Good pruning practices, selecting strong branches with wide-angled crotches that have strong tissue connecting them to the main trunk will minimize this type of injury.

Another threat to fruit is frost pockets, often found in river bottom land or in spots where air cannot flow away on the slope. They will often cause poor fruit set, particularly if frost occurs at pollination time. Apricots and peaches flower earlier and are thus more subject to spring frost injury.

VINE FRUITS

Grape plants have to be protected where temperature falls below -20 to -28°C on a regular basis, as winter injury can occur. Each fall the canes are untied, carefully bent over, layered or pegged on the ground, taking care that they do not break. They are then covered with 7 - 10 cm of soil or, where snowfall is reliable, 15 to 20 cm of straw or hay mulch. In spring remove the mulch before bud break and select 3 - 5 young canes that grew during the previous season. Tie them up to the trellis, trimming back to leave a total of 30 - 60 buds.

GROUND COVER FRUITS

Low winter temperatures injure strawberry roots, crowns and flower buds. Freeze-thaw cycles can lift plants and break roots. Cover plants with straw or hay after light frost has frozen the soul surface, which in the Metro area will be about mid-November. Too early an application can cause leaves and crowns to rot. Remove the covering in early spring when there are signs of new growth, about late April. Straw can be left between the rows to reduce weeds and as a cover if late spring frost threatens.

VARIETIES, PESTS AND OTHER THINGS

TREE FRUITS

Pest and Disease Control • Tree fruits require an extensive spray program to control certain insects and diseases, particularly apple scab disease, which can reduce attractiveness of the crop at harvest time. For gardeners who prefer natural materials to chemicals, Dipel, Rotenone and insecticidal soaps can be used for general insect control. Disease-resistant cultivars of apples, suitable for areas near the lake, include Macfree, Moira, Nova Easygrow and Trent. Caterpillars that attack fruit trees can be controlled by using contact sprays. Tent caterpillars can be hand picked. Mites are tiny spider-like insects which feed on the undersides of leaves and cause foliage to turn bronze during hot dry periods. Use a contact chemical to control them. Regular gathering and destruction of dropped fruit will help to control codling moth on apple and pear trees, but chemical controls during mid-June to mid-August may be required. On apple and pear trees, spots on leaves and later on fruit are caused by scab. The only effective control for this problem is to use protective fungicide sprays during the infection period. Consult your Ontario Ministry of Agriculture and Food extension service for information on timing and materials.

Types To Purchase • Apple varieties suitable for growing in the Metro Toronto area include: Quinte, Yellow Transparent, Tydeman Red, McIntosh, Spartan, Cortland, Idared, Golden Delicious, and Golden Russet.

Pear trees tolerate poor soil conditions, but grow and produce better on good soils. Dwarf pear trees are usually grown on quince rootstocks and are available from nurseries. They grow more upright growth pattern than apple trees, often requiring very little initial training. They are more resistant to scab, thus requiring less disease control. They are susceptible to fireblight, a disease which can easily destroy trees, particularly if they are located near potential sources of infection such as wild apple and pear seedlings, mountain ash and hawthorn. Pear trees suitable for the Metro Toronto area are: Clapp, Bartlett, Flemish Beauty, Anjou and Bosc.

STONE FRUITS

Pests and Diseases • Plums are subject to black knot disease. In early spring, remove black knot cankers by cutting well below the knot to just above a lateral branch or bud. Destroy the cankers since they can be a source of infection via fungal spores if left lying on the ground. Cankers are dangerous lesions on the stems and branches of peach trees. They can be recognized as sunken patches which differ in colour from the surrounding bark; in damp weather, black-, red-, or brown-coloured spores can be seen flowing from them. To reduce the incidence of peach canker on peach trees, prune during a warm dry day, remove dead twigs, cut cankered branches at least 15 cm below any injury and prune annually to avoid the development of cankers on large branches.

Types To Buy • Plum varieties include Early Golden and Burbank. Good peach varieties are Redhaven and Redskin. Tart cherry types include Montmorency, Northstar and English Morello. Sweet cherrieslike Bing, Early Rivers and Viscount, grow only in the warm zone

BUSH FRUITS

Gooseberries and Currants • Berries ripen over a period of two weeks. Yields from gooseberries and red currants will be approximately 5 L per bush, and half that for black currants. Black currant cultivars include Topsy, Baldwin and Consort. Red currant varieties are Red Lake and Cascade. Clark, Fredonia and Captivator are some gooseberry varieties. Insects attacking bush fruit include aphids, can be controlled by insecticidal soaps, and borers, which cause injury to old wood. Cut out shoots older than three years since they are unproductive and more prone to borers.

Raspberries and Blackberries · Raspberries are cane-type fruits; very hardy and easy to grow. They are biennial: they fruit every two years and then die. New canes arise from the plant base and produce fruit the following year. All raspberries are planted in early spring as soon as the soil can be prepared, though red raspberries may be planted in late October or early November. Pick the crop when the fruits have good colour and are firm. Pick frequently; over-ripe berries can attract sap beetles, which lodge in the cores of the canes looking for fermenting juice. Blackberries and black and purple raspberries are treated as red raspberries; however they do not sucker as easily. Red raspberry cultivars include Comet, Newburg, Killarney and Heritage, the latter being fall-bearing. Good purple raspberry varieties are Royalty and Brandywine; black raspberry varieties include Bristol and Cumberland. Blackberry varieties include Darrow and Lowden.

VINE FRUITS

In Toronto's downtown area, hybrid varieties of grapes such as De Chaunac, Vidal and Marechal Foch are hardy. Outside the Niagara Peninsula, the growing season may not be sufficiently long enough to ripen grapes. Select an early maturing variety for the Toronto area.

GROUND COVER FRUITS

The easiest fruit to grow is the strawberry, which can be used as a ground cover in sunny locations. Temperature and day lenght affects the growth of strawberries. Runners are produced in the long warm days of summer, and in the short cold days of fall this stops and flower buds form within the plant crown. Flower clusters emerge and open in May-June. Berries ripen some 4-5 weeks later.

GROWING NUTS

Many nut trees could be used in the design of your property. Black walnut, butternut, heartnut and Persian walnut can be used as shade trees. Filberts and hazel nuts can be used as large shrubs or windbreaks. Nut trees are sensitive to transplantation and should only be purchased as containerized plants in the spring of the year. As with fruit trees, good, well-drained soils with good air drainage result in the best nut crops. The planting process is similar to that of tree fruits. New plantings should be kept weed free, mulched and well-watered during the summer months. Fertilizing as for apples and pears is recommended. Pruning consists of removing dead and diseased branches. Many nut trees possess strong natural forms and. except the black walnut, do not lend themselves to central leader type structure. Harvesting generally consists of picking the nuts in the fall. If squirrels are a problem, check the tree early in the morning and gather the nuts as the squirrels nip them off. Cultivars for the Metro Toronto area include the Persian walnuts Hansen, Nebraska and Himalaya. The latter is much hardier, and better in the northern fringes of Metro. Bates is a heartnut that can be used throughout the city. Butternuts include George Aylmer and the hardier Kenworthy. Black walnuts include Emma Kaye, and Westchoke, a very hardy variety. Chenoka and Laroka are filbert selections.

TREE & SHRUB GARDENING

Trees and shrubs form the matrix of the garden. Deciduous and evergreen trees supply the major vertical elements that define the garden space. Deciduous and evergreen shrubs are intermediate plants that integrate and blend the strong vertical components, like trees and the house, to the horizontal lines of the garden, including its lawns.

THE DIFFERENT FORMS

There are five basic forms in which a tree can be trained: standard, half-standard, low-headed, multi-stemmed and bush. The standard form has a single, straight trunk which is free of branches to a height of 1.8 m. A half-standard tree is similar but has a branch-free trunk to a height of only 0.9 to 1.2 m. Low-headed trees have short trunks, often less than 1 m high. A multi-stemmed tree is a high, medium or, occasionally, low-headed tree with more than one main trunk. The ideal multi-stemmed form has three equally spaced trunks of equal girth and height. More than five trunks tend to make a tree look like a large shrub.

The bush form has several main stems originating at or near ground level, forming a large shrub-like plant.

Forms of Trees and Shrubs

Shrubs can be defined as woody plants, generally of smaller stature than trees, with several main shoots originating at or near ground level. A shrub is usually well branched and carries foliage from top to bottom.

The distinction between a large shrub and a small "bush-form" tree is a bit blurred and arbitrary. Size is the major distinguishing characteristic.

SIZE AND FORM AT MATURITY

In order to plan the placement and effect of trees and shrubs in a garden, it is necessary to know three things: the height, spread and form of the plants when they reach maturity. This data makes it possible to decide what trees and shrubs can be planted and where, how far apart they should be planted to create a specific landscape effect, what will be the predictable future effects of size, shade and root spread on the garden, and what will be the aesthetic effect of the plants on the garden landscape.

DEFINING MATURE SIZE

Define the size of a tree or shrub at maturity is difficult, since each plant grows differently, and soils and gardening techniques vary. A reasonable definition is the approximate size of a nursery grown and formed tree, 25 to 30 years after planting in an urban garden where it received regular watering and good garden care. In the case of a shrub, size at maturity may be defined as the approximate size achieved under a regimen of regular watering and good garden care before old age and/or poor form suggest replacement or rejuvenation pruning.

LOCATION AND PLACEMENT

LANDSCAPE PROBLEMS

Major long range landscape problems stem from inadequate knowledge of size at maturity. These problems can include: planting where there is insufficient space for a plant to mature and produce the garden designer's intended effect; planting trees and shrubs too close together, resulting in overcrowding and excessive shade, etc.; planting too close to houses, walls, fences, pathways, driveways and neighbours' yards; and, as one result of such miscalculations, the need for regular and unnecessary pruning.

Knowing the mature height, spread and form of trees and shrubs before planting will enable you avoid many problems.

OTHER FACTORS

A number of other factors also determine which trees are selected for the home lot. These include hardiness, resistance to insect and disease problems, and structural strength. Structural strength is important since it enables a tree to withstand winter ice and summer windstorms with minimal damage.

SOIL PREPARATION

To grow trees, deeper top-soils than are generally found in home gardens are required. Individual circular "tree-pits" are dug out for each tree, 10 cm deeper and 30 cm wider (all around) than its root system. Save only the topsoil, discarding the clay or gravel subsoil and other debris.

During preparation, remove all perennial weeds, add new top soil as necessary, and thoroughly mix a 5 to 7.5 cm deep layer of organic matter, and 0.5 to 1 kg of 0-20-0 superphosphate, with each m^3 of topsoil. For shrubs, spread a layer of organic matter and rototill into the planting area. Prior to planting, work into the soil, 60 ml of 10-20-20 fertilizer, covering a circular area, four feet in diameter for each plant.

BUYING TREES AND SHRUBS

Since trees and shrubs are a major element in landscape design and a major investment, care should be taken in their selection. Insect, disease and structural problems are also important to consider, and will be discussed later, since they are particular to specific types of shrubs and trees.

BARE ROOT STOCK

Bare root stock is the least expensive form in which to purchase a tree or shrub. It is available in trunk diameters of up to 100 mm. Check for a fibrous, moist root system, plump buds and green branches. Trees with sunken areas on the branches should be avoided, as these may be diseased. Make your purchase early in the season, because most bare root trees are dug in the fall. The later they are planted in the spring, the more likely warm air temperatures will cause leaf growth before the root system has grown enough to support new leaves. Early plantings will establish root growth first, then normal leaf growth.

When transporting a bare root tree home from the nursery, its root system must never be allowed to dry out. The root system should be wrapped in sphagnum moss, wet burlap, or even put into a plastic bag to hold in moisture. Carry the tree home in your car trunk, but if it must be exposed, cover it with burlap to prevent excessive wind damage.

Heeling In
If, a tree cannot be planted immediately, dig a temporary hole for it, remove the wrapping material, place its roots in the temporary hole and cover them with moist soil. Tramp well to eliminate air pockets and water. A tree heeled in on an angle in the shade can be left for a few days, until the final site is prepared.

CONTAINER GROWN AND CONTAINERIZED PLANTS

For later plantings, purchase container grown trees and shrubs. It is important that root disturbance is minimal for specimens planted after the spring season; container grown plants have more established, complete root systems and are more likely to survive the transplanting process. Furthermore, you can see what leaf form and colour you are going to get on your tree or shrub. There are two kinds of container grown plants; true container grown, and containerized.

Container grown • A plant grown in a container for one or more growing seasons is container grown. Its root soil ball has absolute integrity and may be removed from the container without breaking up or losing soil. Container grown plants can be safely planted any time the soil is not frozen.

Containerized • A containerized plant is a plant which has grown in a container for less than one complete growing season. Depending on how long a plant has been in its container, the integrity of its root soil ball may range from good to very poor. If there is little integrity the root soil ball may totally or partially break apart when the plant is removed from its container. The plant may subsequently die or be seriously set back.

TRANSPLANTING LARGE TREES

Large trees moved by tree spade are in vogue today, and although expensive, do give the required instant landscape effect. Certain types such as mountain ash and paper birch, which do not move well in large sizes. Make sure the tree ball is not undersized. A 1.1 m diameter root soil ball is required for a tree with a 10 cm diameter trunk. Look for a 10:1 ratio, root soil ball to trunk diameter.

Conifers (Cone-bearing, needle-leaved evergreens) are sold balled and burlapped, containerized or in wire baskets.

SHRUBS

Shrubs are purchased and planted in the spring, often as bare root specimens. The same precautions used for bare root trees are required for these plants to ensure successful establishment. Most of these bare root specimens come in plastic bags which, if kept closed, can be stored in the refrigerator until planting time. Do not leave the plastic-bagged plants in the sunshine prior to planting — they may heat up and die. Bare root plants may appear dry at the time of purchase. If so, soak the roots in water for 2 to 3 hours before planting.

PLANTING

TIMES TO PLANT

The preferred season for bare root planting is early spring, from the time when frost is out of the soil until deciduous trees and shrubs barely begin to leaf out, generally mid-April to mid-May in Toronto. Stock which has been pre-dug, balled and burlapped, container grown or lifted by tree spade, can be planted later. Late planting enables contractors and homeowners to move trees, shrubs and evergreens during the warmer, drier months, and until freeze-up in late fall. Late fall, after leaf drop, is another favourite period for transplanting bare root deciduous stock. However, there are limitations since some trees and shrubs do not move well in the fall and are generally better moved in the spring

BARE ROOT TREES — PLANTING

Ensure that the tree pit is dug wider than the tree root system. Put some prepared soil in the bottom of the pit and place the tree so that its root system is at the same depth as when growing in the nursery. The previous depth is indicated by a change in bark colour at soil level. On heavy, wet soils, plant the tree slightly higher (7.5 to 10 cm) than in well drained soils. A stake should be placed, avoiding roots and pounded in (see section on support). Fill the hole with prepared soil and tramp well around the roots, to create good root-soil contact. Prepare a slight trough around the tree base to catch and hold water, then water the tree thoroughly. Thereafter, provide 2.5 cm of water at about 10 day intervals, or more often during drought periods.

CONTAINER PLANTING

If there is any doubt as to how long the plant has been in the container, and provided that a plant's container is plastic or metal it may be wise to leave the plant in it for several months before planting, to allow the root soil ball to develop sufficient integrity to permit risk-free planting. Be sure to keep it well watered during this period.

If the container is made of compressed fibre or some other biodegradable material, the plant and container may be planted together using this technique:

- Stand the container in a bucket of water to soak it thoroughly; remove it and allow surplus water to drain away.

- Cut the container rim to be level with the soil.

- If the soil is solid enough that it will not fall out, cut out the bottom of the container.

- Cut four equidistant vertical slashes through the container wall from about 3 cm below its top down to just above its bottom.

- Plant the container no more than 2.5 cm below the soil surface.

- Don't allow any part of an organic container to poke above ground level; like a wick, it draws water from the soil and evaporates it into the atmosphere.

The best times for transplanting coniferous evergreen trees and shrubs are from mid-April to freeze-up. If digging, balling and moving within a garden, never move a tree or shrub when in full growth (mid-June to mid-August).

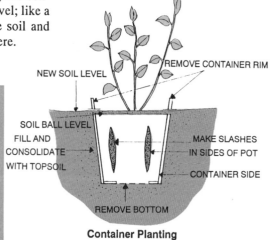

Container Planting

BALLED AND BURLAPPED - WIRE BASKETS

Trees that come in wire baskets, or wrapped in burlap, can be planted in the same way as container-grown plants. However, burlap wrapping should be removed from a tree's roots before it is planted.

SHRUBS

Shrubs do not require the same depth of prepared soil as trees and can be easily planted in normal garden soils which have been prepared for vegetables. They can be planted as soon as the soil is workable.

All perennial weeds must be eradicated before planting begins. Generally, clean cultivation for one growing season prior to planting is sufficient. Where time or patience is limited, consider natural or artificial herbicides. Types and rates are available from local agricultural extension offices.

When planting shrubs, keep the roots moist and/or heel in the plants until the planting pits are ready. Set plants slightly deeper than they were growing in the nursery, then spread out the roots and cover with prepared soil. Tramp well and water thoroughly. At planting time, prune back branches of young shoots to 10 to 15 cm above the soil level.

Control weeds by shallow hoeing and/or mulch with straw or pine bark. Feed each spring with approximately 175 to 225 g of 10-10-10 fertilizer per mature bush: spread the fertilizer under the branches and 30 cm beyond, working it into the soil. Water during the growing season until late August or early September, particularly during droughts.

SUPPORT

Bare root trees will need support for two growing seasons. The stake may be a metal bar or pipe or a 2.5 x 2.5 cm piece of wood, and is placed in the tree pit before the roots are covered. It should be firmly placed on the prevailing wind side of the tree. Following the backfill operation, the trunk of the new tree is tied to the stake either by wire running through old garden hose in a figure of eight, or strips of burlap tied in a similar configuration. Proprietary collars and ties may also be used. Over the next two growing seasons, ties must be checked for tightness around the trunk and loosened if they are cutting into the bark.

Deciduous trees with their root-soil balls in wire baskets are generally heavy enough that the ball will keep the tree upright and in place. Evergreen types require three stakes in a triangular pattern around the trunk. The first stake needs to be leaning into the prevailing wind and the others can be placed equidistant around the trunk.

In the heavy clay soils on the periphery of Metro Toronto, trees should be planted somewhat higher than normal, and should be mulched and watered sparingly. At transplant time, add superphosphate or bonemeal to the topsoil at 28 to 56 g per 36 L of soil; mix in well and backfill. This encourages root development and top growth.

WHICH PLANTS TO PRUNE

A true container grown plant does not require pruning after planting unless it needs training to a specific form. However, bare root plants (unless they have been root-pruned at the nursery) should be pruned, as they have extensive fibrous root systems. When a tree is dug at a nursery, about 75% of its root system is left in the ground. When this happens, the transplanted tree doesn't have enough water gathering power and is unduly stressed. The result is wilting or flagging, loss of some leaves, slow growth, and generally slow recovery from the transplant shock.

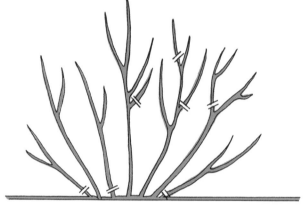

Pruning a Transplant

HOW TO PRUNE

By pruning, the canopy and roots are brought back into balance with some compensation for root loss. Pruning deciduous trees at the time of planting reduces the number of buds (and subsequently leaves). Prune in a manner that results in a good form or shape. This is achieved by removing competing leaders (leaders are strong-growing shoots found at the ends of the main trunk and major framework branches):

• Where two or more leaders develop at the end of the same trunk or major branch, remove all but the strongest leader.

• Remove any laterals arising from the main trunk that are not required as major framework branches.

• Shorten all side branches growing from the major framework branches and leaders to between one third and one half their length, cutting back the least vigorous branches the most.

• Always make cuts just above and sloping back from a bud, natural branch or side shoot that is pointing away from the centre of the tree. Carry out the work immediately after planting or when the tree is completely dormant. Birch, maple and evergreen trees are usually not pruned at planting time.

WATERING

Regular watering is required to establish transplanted trees; for the first week it should be every other day, then it can be reduced to once every 3 or 4 days, and finally to every 10 to 14 days. Beware of summer rains which, while greening up lawns, may not be enough to supply deeper tree roots. Be careful not to overwater in heavy clay soils. Overwatering prevents oxygen from reaching the roots between waterings since the soil does not dry out.

FEEDING

Fertilizing the tree root area when feeding the lawn should be sufficient until the tree is well established. At this stage a 10% nitrogen lawn fertilizer at 0.2 to 0.4 kg per cm diameter of trunk may be spread over the root area in early spring or late fall and watered in. Evergreens and shrubs require 0.5 to 1 kg per 10 m² of bed of a 10% nitrogen fertilizer. Hedges require 0.5 kg per 30 m for small hedges under 1 m high, to 1.5 kg for hedges over 2.5 m high.

HOEING AND WEEDING

Hoe the soil surface around newly planted trees and shrubs with Duch hoe to eliminate seedling weeds and create a surface dust mulsh. Weeds close to trunks and stems should be removed by hand to prevent damage to the bark.

MULCHING

Mulching around the trunks after elimination of grass and weeds aids moisture conservation and controls weed growth. It also prevents damage to tree trunks by monofilament trimmers and rotary mowers.

WINTER INJURY

Transplants and younger trees will require late summer and fall care to reduce the possibility of winter injury. Discontinue watering by mid-September and feeding by early August, otherwise a late flush of growth may not have a chance to harden off prior to winter. Crotch injury happens when the bark cannot withstand the cold and dies, leaving a site for fungal invasion.

Gardens located on the fringes of Metro Toronto and adjacent to open fields may be invaded by field mice and rabbits during the winter months. Be sure that grass around trees and shrubs is trimmed down to eliminate nesting sites, apply additional mulches after the soil is frozen, and place baits where necessary. Metal guards firmly pushed into the soil around a tree trunk will also control mice. From the surface of deep snow, rabbits can reach the lower branches of trees. These portions of the tree should be sprayed with a repellent

PRUNING

Pruning deciduous trees, whether young or mature, requires an appreciation of tree structure, the natural habit of growth for each species, and the purpose the trees are to serve (i.e. lawn specimen, shade tree, street tree or windbreak). It is usually desirable to allow ornamental trees to grow in their natural form with some pruning to correct faults and ensure good form and structure.

As the tree matures, corrective pruning may be required. Sucker growth at the base of the trunk, crossing and poorly spaced branches, and those that form narrow crotches (less than 45°) with the trunk, should be removed. Branches forming wide angles (60° to 90°) with the trunk should be retained so that a strong framework of scaffold branches is established (see diagram on p. 98). The lower branches of most shade and lawn trees should be removed to a height of about 2 m so that there is sufficient clearance for pedestrians to walk beneath them.

Some trees such as the European hornbeam have a naturally low branching habit, so that their branches sweep out from the trunk close to the ground. The natural beauty of such trees depends on this effect; if this type of tree is used, no attempt should be made to remove the lower branches. However, be sure you have enough room before planting small trees.

Pruning Mature Trees • It may be necessary to control the size of a tree after it has reached maturity. Pruning large trees, those over 6 m in height, is not for amateurs. It is recommended that arborists, trained in tree climbing and correct safety procedures from firms with adequate insurance coverage, should be employed for this work. A limb of a tree should not be cut off directly, as this process can tear the bark from the trunk below it. With larger limbs, two preliminary cuts are made before removing them completely. The first cut is on the underside of the limb, about 45 cm from the trunk; the second cut is from the top of a limb, about 5 cm further out, then down and through until the limb drops.

Very large limbs may have to be steadied and lowered with a rope suspended from a higher branch. This is essential if the branch is over a power line, roof, fence and shrub border, or anywhere falling limbs may cause damage. The final cut, to remove the stump, should be made at the branch collar. This is a raised area of growth, close to where the limb and the tree trunk join. The area of the branch collar contains chemicals and cells which promote rapid callous growth and hence faster wound closure. If no branch collar exists, then cut the branch flush with the trunk. If a stub is left it will probably die back because there is no flow of sap through it. This causes decay, which will spread into the trunk and create a cavity.

Pruning Conifers • Coniferous plants may also require pruning to correct faults and to maintain symmetry. Most people consider it a violation to cut back or trim the beautiful new growth of coniferous evergreens, such as junipers, it is a good practice to do so. If the heavy foliage of spreading junipers is allowed to extend out too far, it could encroach on other plants and smother them; the branches are often broken under the strain of heavy snow in winter. In time the centre of the plant becomes open and rather bare, and a sprawling, octopus-like shape results.

MEDIUM PERENNIALS

• Many perennials are in the easy-to-manage, medium height range. Use them to provide short 3-6 week bursts of seasonal colour.

• Use early flowering perennials to bridge the gap between early bulbs and summer perennials. Similarly, use late-flowering kinds to provide a succession of colour throughout late summer and autumn.

False Indigo (Baptisia australis) and Speedwell (Veronica teucrium).

Yellow Loosestrife (Lysimachia punctata), Lulu Lupins and Oriental Poppies.

Plantain Lily (Hosta undulata cultivar) and trunks of European White Birch (Betula pendula).

Purple Cone-flower (Echinacea purpurea) — a medium height perennial.

• Hostas are tough, long-lived, shade tolerant perennials that are well able to compete with the roots of trees and shrubs, making excellent ground covers among such plants. *(above)*

Autumn Stonecrop (Sedum spectabile) — late flowering perennial.

• Many herbaceous perennials will thrive on one application of a complete, balanced fertilizer each year, applied when the new shoots are beginning to show signs of vigorous growth.

• Hoe the fertilizer into the soil surface between plants and "water in" generously.

One of the Sea Hollies (Eryngium spp.) — a long-lived perennial.

Blanbet Flower (Gaillardia aristata) — a cottage garden perennial.

Clustered Bellflower (Campanula glomerata "suberba")—a 1m perennial.

• With perennials, don't put all your eggs in one or two baskets. Don't plant all your early, mid-season or late flowering plants in one spot. Be sure to locate them around the garden so that several clumps of delphiniums, lupins and asters are in bloom throughout the garden at different seasons.

• With perennials, use colours that harmonize or contrast but don't clash. Deep blue and orange is fine, but shocking pink and scarlet may be hard to take.

Golden Groundsel (Ligularia "Sungold") — a large, late-flowering perennial.

One of the variegated, ornamental grasses.

Snow-in-summer (Cerastium tomentosum) — a mat-forming perennial.

• When uniformly spaced in groups, many of the more vigorous, mat-forming perennials can be used to create attractive, carpeting ground covers.

Carpathian Bell-flower (Campanula carpatica " White Clips") — low perennial.

Japanese Star Primrose (Primula sieboldii) — an early, dwarf perennial.

• Low perennials are a very useful group of plants. Plant them towards the front of the border or in masses to form colourful mats.

• Many mat-forming kinds may be under-planted with early-flowering bulbs. The bulbs emerge first, flowering above the foliage mat, and the perennial flowers later, masking the bulb foliage.

Orange Fleabane (Erigeron aurantiacus) — dwarf perennial — and Wooly Yarrow (Achillea tomentosa).

Alpine Pink (Dianthus alpinus) — a dwarf, mat-forming perennial.

Bloody Cranesbill (Geranium sanguineum) — ground covering perennial.

• Low perennials may also be used as border or bed edgings. As long as not too invasive, they are at home in the rock garden.

• A real advantage to low plants is ease of maintenance. Most don't need staking; they cover the ground, crowding out weeds, and need only a light shearing after flowering to encourage dense foliage growth.

FLOWERING SHRUBS

*Purple Smoke Tree (Cotinus coggyria purpureus)
— Handsome coloured foliage shrub.*

• Several shrubs, including the purple foliaged and flowered Smoke Tree, possess coloured foliage including yellow, purple, silver and variegated. These are valuable sources of long term colour. *(left)*

• While hybrid tea, floribunda and polyantha roses provide flowers throughout the summer, do ask your garden centre about the many shrub roses such as Persian Yellow, Altai, Red-leafed, Hansa and other Japanese Roses. *(right)*

• Consider some of the late summer and fall flowering shrubs including the Snow Hills, Pee Gee and Anabelle Hydrangeas. *(below)*

Hansa Rose — An old-fashioned shrub rose.

*Snow Hills Hydrangea (Hydrangea arborescens
grandiflora) A late summer-flowering small shrub.*

• Shrubs form a major part of the permanent living structure of the garden. They are particularly useful in providing bursts of colour, especially during spring and early summer—the period during which many of them flower.

• Two valuable groups of long-season, summer flowering shrubs are the small statured, red-flowering bumalda spireas and the 45-120 cm white, yellow, orange, pink and red flowered varieties of Shrubby Cinquefoil (Potentilla fouticosa).

A Dwarf, native willow (Salix spp.) displaying fine autumn tints.

Snowball Tree (Viburnum opulus) — in fruit during winter.

• Several shrubs exhibit brilliant fall colour.

• In garden planning, don't forget to enrich your late season palette by planting a few strategically located plants with outstanding autumn colour. Outstanding plants include Mountain Ash, Peking Cotoneaster, Euonymus alatus, Pears, Willows, Birch and several Maples including the outstanding Amur Maple.

Burning Bush (Euonymus alatus) — Medium Shrub—excellent fall colour.

Pear Tree (Pyrus sp) in fall colour.

• Don't forget berried plants in your planning. Elders, Bush Honeysuckles, Crabapples, Mountain Ash and Snowball Tree can provide welcome extra late colour through their bright fruits.

European Mountain Ash (Sorbus aucuparia) — a smaller tree in full fruit.

• Since many urban gardens are not large enough to contain many trees, selecting those that flower makes good sense. In this way, multi-use is achieved. The trees not only provide shade, screening, definition, wind buffering and summer foliage, but a short, spectacular burst of flower colour as well.

• Among outstanding flowering trees are Mountain Ash (also heavily fruited and great autumn colour), Flowering Dogwood, Rosybloom Crabapple, Japanese Tree Lilac, Mayday Tree, Ohio Buckey and Schubert Choke-cherry.

Flowering Dogwood (Cornus florida rubra) — a small, early-flowering tree.

Almey Crab-apple, Colorado Blue Spruce and Mayday Tree — a fine spring display.

• Be sure that you have enough room to accommodate the canopy-spread of a tree when it achieves its mature size.

• Flowering trees need to be placed in sunny locations. Too much shade from adjoining trees may inhibit flowering.

Japanese Tree Lilac (Syringa reticulata) — a late-summer-flowering, truly tree-form Lilac.

European White Birch (Betula pendula) — in flower (catkin) in spring.

• While all mature trees produce flowers, many of them are less than conspicuous, such as the catkins of the European Birch and the greenish yellow bracts of the lindens. Since they don't produce what we normally call "flowers", perhaps non-flowering, while not accurate, is appropriate.

• Most non-flowering trees are large shade trees. Great care must be exercised in the placement of large shade trees since they eventually achieve considerable branch spread, resulting in wide-spread shade, and lots of invasive roots. Most urban lots are not able to carry more than 1 to 3 such forest giants.

• In urban gardens, trees are best trained and pruned to develop trunks that do not carry any side branches until 1.8-2.4 m above the ground. This results in a higher head or crown which does not take up space at or just above ground level. Thus the land under trees can be used by people or plants.

Amur Maple (Acer ginnala) — a small tree with exquisite autumn colour.

• Larches are an interesting group of conifers. Unlike most needle-leaved trees they are deciduous, losing their leaves in the fall like oaks and poplars. In the spring distinct clusters of needles emerge from dormant buds producing an early flush of brilliant green. The summer foliage is fine-textured and light green, followed by golden autumn tints.

Siberian Larch (Larix sibirica) — a deciduous, cone-bearing tree.

A trio of Dwarf Mugho Pines (Pinus mugo pumilio) anchoring a large deck (Canoe Birch trunks).

• Excepting trees and shrubs with coloured bark, evergreens are the only plants which truly provide year-round colour.

• Use coniferous evergreens as accent, foundation and background plants.

• Most of the plants with strong, controlled, architectural forms are in this category. Spruce, fir, Western white cedar and Junipers provide pyramidal, columnar, oval, rounded, spreading and ground-hugging forms.

• Coniferous evergreens provide a wide range of subtle foliage colours ranging from the deep green of mugo pine and Alpine Fir through the yellows, greys, silvers and blues of the junipers to the bright blues of Colorado Spruce varieties.

Branden Columnar Cedar (Thuya occidentalis "Brandon". One of the many column-shaped varieties.

Early shortening, by removing the ends of new shoots, is usually the best pruning procedure. A later adjustment can be made by undercutting: removing a main branch just below an overlapping growth. This process ensures that pruning cuts are hidden. Mature, spreading junipers can be reduced in size with this method; however, it is important not to cut back to bare wood, as new buds cannot be regenerated on old wood.

Training New Leaders • Sometimes the leader of a pine or spruce is accidentally broken. A new leader may be trained into place by selecting the strongest side shoot from the upper whorl, bending it up carefully and tying it securely to a stiff stake. Check the tie from time to time to see that it is not biting into the new shoot.

Mugho Pines • Mugho pines differ considerably in form and rate of growth. The most desirable types are the dwarf, multi-stemmed individuals. To maintain compact growth, pruning may be necessary. Normally each branch makes a candle-like growth of 5 to 15 cm early in the year. To control the branch's growth, about half of this candle may be cut off before its new needles elongate; otherwise the plant will grow with a loose habit or shape. This should be done in June when the candle growth is almost complete. At this time, new buds form immediately below where the cut is made. If pruning is deferred until later in the summer, new buds will not form and an unsightly stump will be evident.

Soft Foliage • White cedar, yew and junipers that possess rather soft foliage can be shaped by shearing. This pruning may be done early in the growing season, and again by mid-summer, provided sufficient growth has occurred. This method is primarily employed in formal gardens, for making young trees more dense.

Shrubs • The form most commonly desired for many deciduous shrubs is a low branched plant with the branches originating at the base, or close to it. High branched shrubs soon become leggy and sparse-looking. Pruning is necessary to attain and maintain a strong, dense form, as well as to get the best flower and foliage production.

When to Prune • The time for pruning a shrub is determined by its flowering tim. The spring and early summer flowering shrubs produce their blooms on older wood: i.e. the growth made in the previous year. These shrubs are the most common type. They should be pruned immediately after flowering, but may require different treatment, depending on the bush, because of different growth rates. Some vigorous growers require pruning every year while others may need pruning at two- or three-year intervals. Some may require pruning only occasionally. If berry production is desired, prune only as often as is needed to maintain a reasonable number of strong replacement shoots.

Trimming shrubs to create rounded heads spoils the natural form of the plants. Such indiscriminate shearing destroys much potential flowering wood and encourages more branches at the top of the plant. Pruning done more knowledgeably and selectively will produce denser, more attractive shrubbery.

Forsythias are vigorous growers that tend to become too dense unless some old wood is thinned out annually after flowering. Wood more than two years old should be cut out near the base. This opens up the plant, making more light available to the central shoots. It also encourages the constant development of new branches for subsequent bloom production. Bridalwreath and other early flowering spireas should also be rejuvenated in this manner, although not as frequently. Summer and fall blooming shrubs flower on younger shoots: i.e. those that grow during the current season. These shrubs should be pruned early in spring, before new growth begins. Prune last year's growth back to leave two or four buds near the base. The new growth from these buds will be the shoots from which the flowers are borne. Usually the weakest growths can be removed entirely without impairing flower production.

Rejuvenation • In many gardens, shrubs are left to grow without pruning, until they become high branched, leggy and generally unattractive. The display of bloom on these shrubs is much poorer than from plants that receive normal or even occasional pruning.

Shrubs may be rejuvenated by one of two processes. The drastic treatment is to cut them back close to their bases; this however prevents them from flowering for at least a two year period, and for the first year they are likely to be decidedly unattractive. A better method is to renovate them over a period of three years, by selectively thinning out about one third of the old wood back to their bases each year. Some of the tallest stems remaining can be shortened back to suitable lateral shoots. Eventually all of the old wood will have been replaced by young, healthy branches that will produce the maximum flower effect and desirable shrub form. Renovation of neglected shrubs is best carried out in spring before growth starts, so that new shoots will have a full growing season.

Two shrubs, the yellow-twig and red-twig dogwood, are specifically grown for their bark colour which dulls with age; these can be cut back to within 15 cm of the base in early spring prior to active growth. New growth produces bright yellow and red branches which contrast nicely with the snow in the winter. With these shrubs, this process can be repeated every four or five years. Dogwoods are excellent shrubs on heavy, wet soils.

TYPES OF TREES AND SHRUBS

TREES

Trees for the garden are either deciduous or coniferous. The former lose their leaves in the fall and the latter are evergreen. Deciduous trees are either shade or flowering trees. Shade trees are the group with the greatest diversity of form, leaf texture, colour and bark interest.

Large Trees • The homeowner should avoid large, fast growing trees, as they are more in scale with large open spaces such as parks. Some trees in this group, however, are suitable for Toronto home gardens, including ash, a very hardy native tree which can be quite large at maturity. Red, green, blue and black ash arc available from local nurseries. Suitable types include Fallgold, a black ash, and Patmore and Summit, two green ashes.

Birches • Birches are very popular white-barked trees that can be purchased as multi-stemmed specimens, but they present problems when grown in suburban and urban areas. If they are grown on well drained soils, fertilized and watered regularly, they will survive for twenty-five to thirty years. If neglected they are susceptible to bronze birch borer, an insect that bores into the trunk and kills the upper portions of the tree. Birch leaf miner, a foliage-eating insect, requires prevention or control measures each year. Another problem is that birches tend to bleed copiously, or lose sap, when pruned in late winter or spring. Prune these trees only when they are in full leaf.

Lindens • Linden, or lime trees, are mostly European in origin; they perform well on home lots. The most common species available is little leaf linden, with its characteristic pyramidal shape. Glenleven, De Groot and Greenspire are cultivars, well worth growing. In hot temperatures lindens suffer from leaf scorch when they are located adjacent to brick walls or concrete walks. Gall forming insects also can cause deformed leaves on lindens, but will not kill the trees.

Maples • Maples are a major group of landscape trees, and many are native. The sugar maple, famous for its sap and glorious fall colour, is always worth growing but prefers well drained soils and a good summer water supply. It can become quite large but, because of its upright habit, allows grass to grow close to the trunk. On the heavier clays of north Metro, the native red maple and its cultivars are good choices. Avoid the Norway maple species, as it is an over-planted city tree. Some of its cultivars such as Emerald Queen, Deborah and Harlequin are good choices, as they are more compact. The Harlequin is a particularly attractive tree, exhibiting variegated leaves.

A popular variety that can be grown in sheltered downtown areas is the Japanese maple, available in a number of textural and leaf colour forms. It is also an ideal multi-stemmed tree, a form appropriate for courtyard and patio use. Spring planting is recommended. Maples are relatively free from insects and diseases.

Oaks • The mighty oaks, red, white and burr, are slow to become established but can grow quite large. They should only be planted in spring. The upright cultivar of English oak is a narrow accent tree that can also be used for screening, since it retains its leaves all winter until the new buds open the following spring.

Others • A native trees are available that are particularly attractive either in leaf shape or fall colour, but can be difficult to transplant successfully. These are Kentucky coffee tree, walnut, butternut. and tulip tree. All these would be hardy in zone 6.

COMPACT FLOWERING TREES

Crabapples • Flowering crabapples form the largest group of compact flowering trees. They come in many forms, from weeping to upright, and have white, pink or red flowers in early spring. Pruning flowering crabs is similar to the pruning process for shade trees except, as with all early flowering trees and shrubs, they should be pruned immediately after flowering.

For all plants in the rose family, insects and diseases are a problem. Aphids, sapsucking insects, may require chemical spray controls such as systemic insecticides, although natural predators such as ladybird beetles do reduce infestations. Apple scab disease is a worse problem and can often cause early defoliation on varieties such as the Almey crab. A number of selections are disease resistant, including the Siberian, Japanese, Sargent and Dolgo crabapples.

Cherry Trees • Other flowering trees in the rose family include Japanese and European cherries. Japanese cherry trees are not long-lived, even in protected areas, and are susceptible to winter injury and subsequent canker diseases. European cherry is a much hardier plant but is susceptible to black knot, a disease common to our native chokecherry. This disease can be controlled by judicious spring pruning. The hardiest types available are the Amur, Sargent and Shubert cherries, all of which are single flowered and hardy in the Metro area.

Ash • Ash prefer well drained soils and full sun and in general are relatively free of diseases and insect problems.

The colourful fruited mountain ash is an ideal size for the home lot but is plagued by sawflies, which eat its leaves, and fireblight. Fireblight is a particularly bad bacterial disease which affects flowers, leaves and branches, often causing the trunk to split and ooze bacterial sap. There is no cure for this particular disease. Pruning out infected parts is recommended; however in my experience, this does not solve the problem. A tree is continuously infected with fireblight from nearby sources, and the trees ultimately deteriorate. European mountain ash and white beam trees are particularly affected.

Hawthorns • The final member of the rose family, the hawthorn, is a popular flowering tree but again, subject to insects, leaf spot diseases and rust. The most disease resistant hawthorn is Washington, a native type which produces berries that persist well into the winter. Hawthorns are notoriously difficult to transplant.

Others • Other flowering trees include horse chestnut and catalpa. The former flowers very early in the season and the latter in mid-summer.

CONIFERS

Conifers or cone bearing trees are evergreens except for two species, Larch and dawn redwood, which lose their needles in the fall. Conifers may be used as windbreaks, specimens or accent trees. Major types are cedars, junipers, firs, pines and spruces.

Cedars • The Eastern white cedar, commonly used for hedges, is native to Ontario. It is available in many forms, from narrow pyramidal to globes. Cedars can tolerate a wide range of soils and temperature extremes. Leaf miner can be a problem but is relatively easy to control.

Junipers • Upright junipers are used for foundation plantings and are compact enough to serve as windbreaks and privacy screens on small lots. All too often pines and spruces that reach a height of 18 m are used in this situation. Upright junipers are a better choice: they reach heights of 4.5 to 6 m and spread approximately 3 m. They are easy to control by light pruning, and are available in a variety of textures and needle colours. Mountbatten, Spartan and Fairview are green cultivars; the scopulorum types, like Wichita Blue, Springbank and Iowa, exhibit colours of silver to blue. Skyrocket is a popular narrow upright, accent-type juniper.

Pines • Sandy, well drained soils are a requirement for pines, the exception being the Austrian Pine, Pinus nigra, much planted in Ontario. This pine is very susceptible to diplodia tip blight, which ultimately kills the tree. Control involves consecutive sprays with a protective fungicide during the development of new growths. Scotch and white pine are large trees that prefer spring planting. In favoured areas near the lake, slower growing pines such as Korean and Swiss stone could be used. Insects that attack pines include pine shoot moth, pinesaw fly and pitch mass borer.

Spruces • In heavier soils, spruces are often substituted for pines. The most popular spruce grown and planted in Metro Toronto is Colorado Blue Spruce and its cultivars: Hoops, Koster and Moerheim. Slow growing blue spruce require space to develop; do not plant them close to the house. There are numerous forms of dwarf spruces such as nest and hedgehog spruce and the dwarf Alberta spruce for rock garden and foundation planting. Spider mites may be troublesome on spruce and junipers during hot dry summers; insecticidal soaps will control these sapsucking pests.

Spreading Junipers • The most common evergreens grown by the nursery industry are spreading junipers. Mass planted, they make effective ground cover plants.

Spreading junipers fall into three broad groups based on their height and spread at maturity. The largest, with the greatest spread, are the Chinese cultivars: Golden Pfitzer and Ramlosa. Compact forms of the Chinese juniper include Old Gold, Compact Pfitzer and Blue Sargents.

The intermediates are basically the Savin group, most of which have a mound-shaped form, except the Savin itself which is vase-shaped. They are excellent for foundation plantings. Savin juniper is probably the most shade-tolerant. The varieties Arcadia, Blue Danube and Tam (or Tamarisk) juniper belong to this group.

The lowest are the horizontalis group. These exhibit a range of blue to blue-green foliage colours are ideal as low ground covers, to a height of 15 to 30 cm. Bar Harbour, Andorra and Blue Rug are commonly grown selections.

Yews • For shady situations, Japanese yews and their hybrids with the European yew are available in mounded, vase-shaped forms. Golden Japanese Yew has unusual gold foliage; Hick's Yew is a narrow growing type, suitable for hedges.

BROAD LEAF EVERGREENS

Broad leaf evergreens are, in general, lovers of acidic soils. In most of Metro Toronto they require special conditions to be successfully grown, which are mentioned below under rhododendron culture. A few types grow easily in ordinary garden soils: boxwood, for instance, is a slow growing hedge plant.

Bearberry Cottoneaster and its cultivars Coral Beauty and Skogholm grow well in sunny, dry areas, but may lose their evergreen foliage where they grow above the snow cover. Mahonia or Oregon Grape and winter creeper are versatile plants that can tolerate sun and shade. The purple leaf type of winter creeper makes a great ground cover while shrubby types such as Emerald Gaiety, Gold Tip and Sunspot provide bright yellow or gold accents.

Rhododendrons and Azaleas • Sheltered and shaded from the wind and sun, broad leaf evergreen rhododendrons and deciduous azaleas can be grown in the Metropolitan area. A site that has a north or east orientation is required, with a soil pH of 4.0 - 6.0. Raised beds containing baled, acid peat can be used. These plants are shallow rooted. Thus a bed 40-50 cm deep should suffice. Ensure that the site is well drained; if necessary, dig down to the subsoil to improve drainage. Plant in spring and water thoroughly and frequently during the growing season. Acid mulches such as oak leaves or pine needles can be added for winter protection. Weeds must be controlled by very shallow hoeing since the root systems of these plants grow near the soil surface. Spent blooms are removed carefully and immediately after the flowers fade, so that growth buds immediately below them are not injured. This prevents seed formation and encourages new growth.

SHRUBS

The lowly shrubs are much misunderstood and little used landscape plants. Shrubs are planted and treated much as trees but reach maturity at an earlier age. They can supply texture, form, colour, flower and fruit, to enhance the total landscape. For covering large areas at a reasonable price there is nothing better than shrubs; many of them are also relatively free of insect and disease problems.

The earliest shrubs to bloom is the flowering quince which produces red to white flowers and large fruit that ripens in the fall, which is also an attraction. Deutzia and mock orange produce white, fragrant flowers in late May; the former may be smaller in size and the latter are generally more upright. One of the earliest flowering shrubs in the Metro area is forsythia, which presents bright yellow flowers on coarse textured shrubs from late April to mid-May. Varieties bred and selected for flower hardiness, Northern Gold and Ottawa, are more reliable in the outer fringes of Metro. Hydrangea is one of the few shrubs to flower in the shade and produces dish-sized white blooms in late summer. Annabelle, Hills of Snow and Peegee are popular varieties.

Honeysuckles are easy to grow but subject to aphids which can disfigure the growing tips. Their red tubular flowers attract hummingbirds. White to yellowish blooms are found on Morrow's honeysuckle, a variety which is quite drought tolerant.

Golden Ninebark and its dwarf form Dart's Gold are native shrubs with attractive golden foliage and reddish brown seed heads. The easiest and most drought tolerant native shrub is shrubby cinquefoil, a low growing, sun loving shrub that exhibits white, yellow or reddish flowers all summer. Abbotswood is a white cultivar, Goldstar and Goldfinger are yellow. Spireas are another group that provide compact plants of early and mid-season flowering. Garland and Snow

White are cascading white flower types in early June; Anthony Waterer and japonica are red to pink midsummer flowering types. Dwarf types such as Little Princess and Shirobana are also available.

Viburnums • Diversity is a feature of the viburnums: early flowering shrubs such as Korean Spice, Burkwood and Fragrant Viburnum grow easily in sun or partial shade. Fruit for birds is provided by the late flowering types such as Wayfaring Tree and Highbush Cranberry.

Roses • Roses such as hybrid teas, floribunda, grandiflora and miniatures can be grown in the Metro Toronto area to provide the perfect blooms expected of the rose. However, to grow them well, an intensive care program is required. Roses are purchased in spring and transplanted much the same as shrubs. If they are in containers, be careful when removing them, as they are generally freshly potted and have a sparse root system. If plants exhibit new white shoots from being in dark cool storage areas, keep them in a shady, sheltered area so that the new shoots can green-up and harden- off before being planted in the open. Well drained, heavy clay soils are suitable for roses but will need the usual organic amendments, as explained in *Chapter 3*. Choose a sunny, sheltered site for planting bushes. Spacing should be approximately 0.9 to 1.2 m apart for grandifloras and hybrid teas can be somewhat closer. Tamp the soil firmly and water well.

Insects and diseases are serious threats to roses and careful spray programs are required to control them. Dormant applications prior to leafing out and fungicides to control black spot are required every 10 to 14 days during the growing season. Since they are not winter hardy, roses will require winter protection. In late fall prior to freeze-up, earth is hilled around the bases of the roses covering as much of the lower stems as possible and, on top of this, a mulch of straw, hay or even pine bark is applied. Any growth above the snow line during the winter is liable to be killed. In spring the protective earth and mulch covers can be removed as soon as the roses appear to be budding. Then pruning commences. Generally, remove dead and brown branches down to the nearest out-facing bud. These new buds will be the first to flower in the coming summer. Later buds that break from lower down will provide later blooms throughout the summer months.

Shrub roses are much hardier than the aforementioned types and generally do not require winter protection; many new disease resistant, winter-hardy types are available and are often termed "landscape roses." The rugosa types — Max Graf, Theresa Bugnet, and Hansa — are suitable for home gardens. The explorer series — David Thompson, Henry Hudson and Jens Monk — are also available. Ground cover roses include Darts Dash and Red Max Graf. Shrub roses are pruned very similarly to other shrubs.

Vines are woody perennial plants that climb or spread over the soil. Add to the vertical element of garden design by training them over fences, house walls, arbours and pergolas. Some, such as Boston Ivy and Virginia Creeper, are grown for foliage effects; others such as Clematis and Climbing Hydrangea for their summer bloom.

CHAPTER 9

LAWNS

Lawns are made up of many grass plants growing very closely together, actively competing with each other for space, nutrients and water. They are capable of living for up to one hundred years. This is why lawns should be constructed with considerable care. There is only one opportunity to do the job properly: the first time. Once a lawn has been sown there is really nothing that can be done to improve inadequate soil preparation, short of reconstruction.

After construction, a careful maintenance program is necessary to ensure the longevity and good health of a lawn.

THE SITE

DRAINAGE

The lawn site must be well drained. Water should not stand in pools on the soil's surface for more than a few hours after heavy rains. Water from spring snow melt should quickly drain down through the subsoil after the soil has thawed. Additional information about drainage may be found in *Chapter 3*.

WEED CONTROL

Prior to grading or soil preparation it is important to eliminate all perennial weeds from the proposed site. Light populations of weeds may be controlled by cultivation (working the soil), but if the land is heavily infested or if there is not sufficient time for cultivation, the use of a weed killer will be necessary.

The better herbicides for broad spectrum weed control contain glyphosphate. When sprayed on the green shoots and leaves of most plants, glyphosphate will kill them. It kills both broad leaved weeds and grasses, but becomes neutralized upon contact with the soil. Consequently, as soon as it has killed the weeds, crops and lawns can be sown. It is best applied as a low pressure, large droplet spray. A small hand sprayer gives the most control. Do not spray when windy. Protect nearby plants with paper or burlap. If in doubt, wash them off with clean water after spraying.

Glyphosphate must be used with great care, strictly in accordance with the directions found on the package. Do not let it run down slopes onto other plants. Just a touch on a green shoot or leaf can kill a plant, do not step in the solution and then walk on a lawn.

For best control, spray when weeds are lush and green: about 15 cm high. After spraying; the weeds will slowly and gradually turn yellow, then brown, at which point the soil may be cultivated.

GRADING

It is important to develop a uniform depth of top soil, overlying a reasonably uniform depth of subsoil, in order to construct a lawn of even texture and colour. If a reasonably level or gently rolling lawn is desired but the site is undulating, it may be necessary to grade the area.

The first step to grading is to move the top soil to one side of the site, just off the area to be constructed. Then shape the subsoil to create the surface grades and contours you want for your lawn. Apply a 5 cm layer of peat moss over the subsoil and work it in thoroughly, 23 to 30 cm deep. Re-spread the top soil to follow final surface contours and grades.

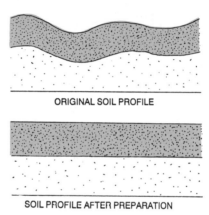

ORIGINAL SOIL PROFILE

SOIL PROFILE AFTER PREPARATION

Grading Lawns

Slopes • Except for larger scale, contoured lawns, construct slopes at less than 15%, or 15 cm vertical over 1 m horizontal.

The maximum safely mowable slope is 30 cm vertical over 1 m horizontal. The minimum slope to ensure adequate surface drainage is 1%, or 1 cm in 1 m, for sites with soil that drains well. A 2% slope, which slopes 2 cm in 1 m, is necessary for sites with poor drainage.

Terraces • Terraced lawns are an excellent way to develop sloping land. They add strong visual interest to the landscape and provide definition and enclosure to garden spaces. Whenever possible be sure to exploit differences in elevation by terracing.

Matching Elevations • Where lawns are planned to abut pathways and other paved areas, leave the final soil level 1 to 3 cm above the hard surface so that, after settling, the lawn will be at or a little above the elevation of the hard surface. Few sights in a garden look more untidy than ragged grass edges, growing above or below a paved area.

SOIL PREPARATION

General considerations and methods are discussed in *Chapter 3*. When constructing lawns, top soil preparation should be carried out with considerable care. For a healthy, vigorous lawn, a minimum depth of 15 to 23 cm of well prepared top soil is required. For sodded lawns this depth includes the thickness of the sod.

Use granular, sphagnum peat moss as the source of organic matter. Apply a 2.5 cm layer over the soil surface for every 10 cm depth of top soil to be cultivated. Do not exceed this amount, or a spongy rather than resilient lawn will result. Next, apply 3 kg of 11-48-0, or 4 kg of superphosphate, for every 100 m² of area to be constructed. Thoroughly mix the peat and fertilizer into the top soil. Consolidate the top soil by heeling: walking over the land in closely spaced rows on your heels, with your toes turned up. Remember that freshly dug soil will lose about 20% of its height as it becomes settled.

PLANTING

Grass is either grown from seed or laid out in sod form. Both techniques are described here in detail.

SEED SOWING

Seed Bed Preparation • Using a good quality steel rake, rake and cross-rake the area to develop a uniform, 3 to 5 cm deep layer of fine, granular soil particles. Remember, the job is not complete until you have achieved the final, finished lawn surface grade. Also bear in mind that short of re-seeding or re-sodding, there's little that can be done to correct unsatisfactory surface grades after the grass is established.

Seeding • Most seed mixtures are sown at a rate of 2 kg per 100 m² of lawn area. Kentucky Bluegrass is sown at a rate of 0.5 to 1 kg per 100 m² of lawn area.

It is of paramount importance to sow evenly and uniformly. When hand sowing this is more easily achieved by mixing the seed with 3 to 5 times its bulk of sand, vermiculite, perlite or fine, dry soil as a spreader. It's much easier to spread a larger volume evenly. First, sow half the seed over the entire area in a north-south direction, then sow the other half in an east-west direction.

There is also a wide range of mechanical spreaders available for purchase or rent. The rotary plate type spreads very evenly and is easy to use. A hand held model is adequate for seeding and fertilizing in the average urban garden. After sowing, rake over the area gently and shallowly in one direction only. Its a mistake to bury the seed too deep. To shade the soil surface from direct sun and excessive drying, and to encourage quick sprouting, a little chopped straw may be scattered over the surface. It can later be chopped up by the mower, after the grass is well established.

Things To Remember
- *Cut out any weeds in the sod with a sharp knife and plug the resulting holes with sod or soil.*
- *It is not necessary to use a roller to compact the sod after laying it.*

SODDING OR TURFING

Preparation • Grading and soil preparation are the same as for seeding, with one exception. There is no need to develop a fine seed bed. Simply rake and cross-rake until the required surface levels are achieved, and the soil is fine enough to bed the sod in intimate contact with the soil surface.

Purchasing • Sod should be healthy and dense, with grass that is medium to dark green in colour and mowed to the correct height. The sod should exhibit plenty of moist roots and should hold together easily when unrolled and shaken. It should be uniform, 3 to 4 cm thick, and free from weeds like quack grass and pests and diseases.

LAYING

The Plank Method • Starting at one end of the area to be sodded, lay a row of sod across the area and a few metres up the sides (see diagram). Tightly butt each section of sod up to its neighbours, and lay the sod 2.5 cm or so beyond the final margins of the lawn area. This permits cutting back to form a clean, sharp edge after the sod has knitted. Lightly pat the sod to ensure contact with the soil surface: standing on the plank will ensure intimate contact. Place a wide plank on the first row of sod. Standing on the plank, facing the bare soil, lay the next row of sod in front of the plank. Lay the sod in a brickwork-like pattern, staggering all the joints. Flip the plank forward onto the second row of sod and stand on it to lay the next row of sod. Continue the procedure until the entire area is covered. With this method, you avoid compacting the soil to be sodded, and all the raking and re-raking that many unreflective gardeners go through.

To transport sods to the area being sodded, place planks across the laid sod to the laying plank. Use a wheelbarrow to carry the sods. Place the rolled sods on the bare soil just in front of the laying plank.

Care After Laying • Water the sod immediately after laying it, and continue to water it frequently so it stays moist but not soggy. When the sod has knitted and is beginning to grow, reduce the frequency and increase the volume of watering. When the grass has grown to about three inches high, begin routine cutting and maintenance. After the sod is well knitted and growing, a light rolling may be given but is not necessary.

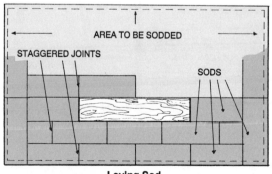

Laying Sod

If your objective is a lush, green, self healing lawn, a routine lawn maintenance program is essential. This is not to say that a reasonable lawn can't result from a less than comprehensive program. Only you can set an acceptable standard.

MOWING

Mowing is a most important operation that strongly affects the quality of a lawn.

First Cut — Following Seeding • As soon as the new grass is about 10 cm high, it may be topped by cutting it to 7.5 cm high. During subsequent cuts, lower the height of cut by 1.25 cm per cut, until the regular cutting height for the grass variety is reached.

Height of Cut • Unlike most other plants, the region of active growth and elongation on grasses is near the base of the shoots. To avoid cutting off these regions of growth, it is necessary to cut the grass at the right height.

Height of cut is measured by placing the mower on a hard, level surface and measuring the distance between the cutting blade or bed bar and the hard surface.

Cutting at the right height is most important for many reasons. It increases the rate of shoot growth, therefore increasing the lawn's density. It reduces the width of leaf blades, resulting in a more finely textured lawn. Eventually, cutting will improve the self healing properties of the lawn.

The correct height of cut for Kentucky Bluegrass is 2.5 to 4 cm.

Frequency • Failing to cut often enough is a common cause of poor quality lawns. They should be cut:

• every 3 - 4 days during the flush of early growth in spring and early summer

• every 5 - 7 days during summer; or a bit less often when the weather is very hot

• once in 10 - 14 days as the weather cools and growth slows in the fall.

As a general rule of thumb, don't allow more than 5 cm of new growth to develop between cuts.

Mowing Hints
• *Keep your mower sharp. Sharp cuts heal cleanly and quickly, resulting in quick recovery and fast subsequent growth. Ragged cuts result in slow healing and recovery, and also give the lawn a brownish cast.*
• *Do not cut wet grass unless it is absolutely necessary.*
• *Always remove grass clippings, to minimize the buildup of thatch at ground level .*

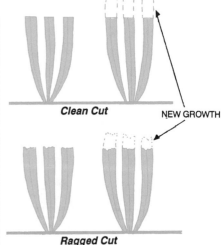

Clean Cut

NEW GROWTH

Ragged Cut

If you go on vacation and the grass gets very long, cut it first at 7.5 to 10 cm high. Reduce the height of cut by 1.25 to 2 cm on each subsequent cut until you are back to the regular cutting height.

FERTILIZING

A regular program is needed on lawns. Ideally, 2 kg of nitrogen per 100 m² of lawn area should be applied during each growing season: 0.5 kg per month in May, June, July and August. Three 0.5 kg applications is the minimum necessary except in areas of regular, heavy rainfall where less nitrogen may be needed. Approximate timing for three applications, is: immediately following spring raking, just as new growth gets under way, in early July and again in late August.

Caution should be exercised after mid-August. Late fertilizing with lots of nitrogen, especially if warm temperatures prevail for several weeks, can stimulate late growth that may be damaged by fall frosts, affecting the winter hardiness of the lawn. Finding out local conditions and practices is best.

To calculate the weight of a specific fertilizer to provide 1 kg of N, divide 100 by the percentage of N it contains. Using 16-20-0 as an example, 100 / 16 = 6.25 kg. In other words, 6.25 kg of 16-20-0 fertilizer will supply one kilogram of actual nitrogen.

Professional Ratios • Professional greens-keepers in golf courses and sports grounds have developed preferences for certain fertilizer ratios.

Some ratios preferred by professional greens-keepers include: 4:1:2, 3:1:2, 2:1:1, 4:1:1, and 5:1:2. Even though there is some variation in levels of phosphorous (P) and potassium (K), the nitrogen (N) is relatively high in most ratios.

Bear in mind that ratios are not the same as percentages. For example fertilizers with percentages 1-2-3, 2-4-6, 3-6-9, and 4-8-12, are all examples (multiples) of the ratio 1:2:3.

Technique • Before applying your fertilizer, calculate and measure the amount needed. In order to promote an even rate of growth, and a uniform colour, apply the fertilizer evenly across your lawn. This may be achieved by using the methods described for seeding.

WATERING

Newly Seeded Lawns • On established lawns, the general rule is to water copiously when water is needed, leaving as long a time as practical between waterings. This encourages deep rooting and promotes drought resistance.

However, this rule does not apply when watering a newly seeded lawn. Prior to seed sprouting, frequent and light watering with a fine spray is needed. Be careful not to create puddling, or to erode the soil surface. The aim is to maintain a uniformly moist but not soggy soil surface, to promote maximum and even seed germination.

Watering
To avoid burning the grass, don't overlap areas when applying fertilizer, and do not dump it in piles. Apply to a dry lawn, water in immediately afterwards.

After germination, when the young grass plants are well rooted, watering can become less frequent and volume of water distributed can be increased, gradually reinstating the general rule.

Regular Watering • During the growing season lawns need 2.5 cm of water every 7 - 10 days, through rainfall or watering. A good watering will penetrate at least 23 cm deep.

Use a good quality sprinkler that produces a reasonably fine droplet and a has slow rate of application, to ensure deep watering without puddling and loss by run-off.

To measure the rate of application, place several tin cans on the grass within the spread of the sprinkler to be tested. Turn on the water. When the water in the bottom of a can is 2.5 cm deep, that particular area has received 2.5 cm of water. This method indicates any variations in volume at different points under the sprinkler.

Remember that frequent, shallow watering encourages the development of shallow rooted grass plants susceptible to drought, as well as weeds and moss.

Indicators • Signs that watering is needed include:

• dry surface soil, 1.25 to 2 cm deep

• wilting grass leaves

• leaves turning a darker green colour, especially in varieties of Kentucky Blue-grass.

FALL WATERING

In some areas, the ground freezes solid during winter but rainfall is absent or too light to penetrate the soil and snow cover is scanty. In these cases late fall watering may be indicated. The objective is to water the soil to its capacity just prior to final freeze up. All soil particles will be well coated with water but free water will have drained away leaving air spaces between soil particles.

WEED CONTROL

The development of a healthy lawn through a sound maintenance program is the primary means to prevent weeds from becoming established. Inevitably, however, a few will still get into the lawn.

For just a few weeds, hand picking and spot treatments may be all that's needed. Watering a day or two before hand picking will soften the soil making the job easier. Be sure to pull or dig up as much root as possible. Raking prior to mowing helps to tear out creeping weeds and sets up weed foliage ready for the mower. Correct watering practices also help to reduce weeds, especially the establishment of weed seedlings.

Chemical Control • Most lawn herbicides contain plant hormones. These are absorbed through the leaves of weeds, then they move throughout the plant and slowly cause grossly distorted growth. In a sense the plant grows itself to death. Bear in mind that, basically, herbicides kill only broad leaved weeds. Apart from

Creeping Bent grasses, which they can damage, lawn herbicides don't kill lawn grasses. This is why they are known as selective herbicides. However, they can kill or at best seriously damage all broad leaved, woody and herbaceous plants. So use with them great care!

Commonly used selective herbicides include 2,4-D amine, Mecoprop and Dicamba. The 2,4-D amine is used to control dandelion, broadleaf plantain and many other broad leaved weeds. It is not as effective as others in controlling clover and chickweed, although repeated applications can take their toll on these two invasive weeds. Mecoprop is used against broadleaf plantain, chickweed, ground ivy, prostrate knotweed and white clover. Dicamba controls prostrate knotweed and white clover.

The best clover and chickweed killers are very effective general lawn herbicides that will kill a broad spectrum of lawn weeds.

Application • Fertilizing a week ahead of applying herbicides will stimulate weed growth, thereby improving the herbicide's effectiveness.

Spray on a warm, still, dry day when the temperature is above 70°F (22°C) and below 80°F (27°C) and the wind speed is less than 6 km per hour. Ideally the soil should be moist and the weeds growing vigorously.

When spraying, don't allow any spray to drift onto plants located adjacent to the lawn. If in doubt, wash bordering plants with water immediately after spraying. To protect plants, cover them with paper or plastic prior to spraying.

Wear a long-sleeved shirt and long pants when spraying, and keep the spray away from your face and bare skin. Don't inhale spray. Wash all exposed skin or take a shower after spraying.

When applying these herbicides, the following practices are suggested:

• follow the directions on the package
• don't be tempted to use spray solutions in a stronger formula than is recommended: remember, a slow kill is the best response
• use low pressure in the sprayer to minimize the problem of drifting
• keep the spray directed downward and close to the lawn
• apply evenly and don't miss any weeds

Don't store herbicides with live plants or fertilizers. Several fertilizers and absorb herbicide fumes. Use separate sprayers for herbicides and other pesticides.

Weed Bars • Herbicide impregnated wax weed bars are also effective and easy to use. For best effect the temperature should be above 70°F (22°C) but not too hot. Check the label for a maximum temperature. Drag the bar slowly over the lawn, slightly overlapping each strip covered to make sure that coverage is complete.

Pesticide Notes
• *If it rains within 24 hours of spraying, it may be necessary to re-spray.*
• *After spraying, wash out the sprayer with detergent and rinse three times with clean water.*
• *Keep your weed control chemicals in tightly closed, well labelled containers, preferably under lock and key.*

Quack Grass • Using glyphosphate, it is possible to get rid of this invasive weed grass in a lawn. There are two approaches: to spray the infested patches of lawn, or to apply a solution of glyphosphate to the tips of the quack grass leaves.

Spraying the infested patches of lawn kills both quack and lawn grasses. One week later, the bare spots can be seeded or sodded.

Applying glyphosphate directly to the quack grass leaves should be done after it has been allowed to grow 7.5 to 10 cm above the tops of the lawn grasses. Using a soft brush or cloth-wrapped piece of wood, very carefully apply a solution of glyphosphate to the tips of the quack grass only. Be sure not to drip any on the lawn. Special applicators that look like hockey sticks are available in garden centres.

Crab Grass • Crab grass usually grows in thin, unwatered lawns, and becomes very prevalent during hot, dry summers. It can be controlled by applying pre-emergent herbicides in the spring.

RAKING

In climates with long cold winters where temperatures seldom rise above freezing for several months and summers are dry, thatch may be a problem. This is a layer of un-decomposed organic matter on the soil surface of a lawn. If not removed it can accumulate to the degree where the grasses root into it, resulting in a shallow-rooted, drought-susceptible lawn. Thatch can impede the absorption of water and fertilizers. It also causes a lawn to become thin and open with a spongy rather than resilient surface.

Early each spring when the lawn is dry enough to walk on without damaging soil texture, it should be thoroughly raked and cross-raked to loosen and remove all thatch. This can be achieved by hand, using a steel-tined rake, or with a vertical cutting power mower.

SCARIFYING

This is the practice of shallow raking to loosen just the soil surface of a lawn. A hand rake or vertical cutting power mower may be used. It is carried out when over-seeding a lawn.

It is also used frequently on bentgrass golf and bowling greens to sever over-ground runners prior to top dressing — a practice seldom seen in the average home garden.

AERIFYING

Aerifying is the practice of making slits or narrow holes in the top few centimetres of a lawn. The basic purpose is to relieve soil compaction on heavily used lawns. The resultant slits or holes shatter the soil a little, allowing easier penetration of air, water and fertilizer. Aerifying improves surface drainage, reduces surface run off and improves root development. The release of trapped carbon dioxide and toxic gases is also facilitated.

Slicing is easily and quickly carried out. Since it disturbs the lawn surface only slightly, it does not interfere with normal lawn maintenance.

Hollow tine aerifying results in small, narrow holes in the lawn and lifts small cores of soil, laying them on the lawn surface. These cores are then broken up and scattered by raking or dragging a flexible steel doormat over the lawn. Ideally the cores should be raked up and removed, and then the lawn should be top dressed and fertilized.

Aerifying may be carried out any time during the growing season, preferably a day or two following a heavy rain or watering when the ground is soft and easily penetrated.

Appropriate equipment is easily rented or a contractor may be hired.

TOP DRESSING

The application of soil, organic matter and sand or mixtures of these materials to a lawn surface is called top dressing. This practice can:

- help to control thatch by accelerating natural decomposition
- level a lawn surface by filling in minor hollows
- improve the drainage and texture of the soil surface
- encourage grass plants to produce more tillers or basal shoots, thereby increasing lawn density
- serve as a mild fertilizer
- act as a carrier for concentrated fertilizers
- follow hollow tine aerifying, to improve the soil structure and fertility
- provide a measure of winter protection

On a level, well constructed and maintained lawn, top dressing will seldom be needed. However, it is not likely to do any harm if properly done.

For general purposes, a mix of four parts medium loam, one part sphagnum peat moss and one part coarse, gritty sand is satisfactory. It should be passed through a 1 cm screen to remove lumps and stones. Ideally, a top dressing compost should be similar in composition to the underlying lawn soil.

Before applying, cut the grass. Use 0.1 to 0.6 m^3 per 100 m^2 of lawn area, spreading it evenly over the lawn. A rule of thumb is never to apply more than a 0.5 cm deep layer at lawn soil level per application. Deeper layers can cause the grass to rot and may asphyxiate the grass plants. Using a stiff broom, the back of a rake or a drag mat, work the top dressing down between the grass blades to the soil surface level.

There is seldom any need to apply sand or organic matter alone. Sharp sand may improve surface drainage on clay soils. A very light dressing of well rotted, crumbly, finely broken manure can provide a mild stimulant, especially when applied after hollow-tine aerifying.

ROLLING

The only justification for this practice is to settle a lawn surface that may have heaved after a hard, frosty winter. Its use is to be discouraged in maintaining home lawns.

RENOVATION

Before considering renovation, check the depth and condition of the top soil. If it's not adequate to support a good lawn, reconstruction is indicated.

Here is a sequence of steps to follow when renovating a lawn. First spray with a selective lawn herbicide to eliminate all weeds. Then cut the grass to about 2.5 cm high and thoroughly rake it to remove all thatch. Hollow tine aerify and remove all cores. Next, top dress with a general compost. Apply 10-30-10 or similar fertilizer at 5 kg per 100 m² of lawn surface area, and water the lawn copiously. Follow up with a full, routine maintenance program.

TYPES OF GRASSES

In the Metro Toronto area three types of turf grasses are grown. Kentucky Bluegrass is used most often. Creeping Red Fescue and some of the other fescues are used for blending, and Perennial Ryegrass serves as a nurse crop, to protect other small grass seedlings.

Kentucky Bluegrass is a common choice in and around Toronto because it naturally adapts to alkaline soils and forms rhizomes, or underground shoots, and deep roots which forage for extra moisture and provide storage for food. Because its roots prevent it from tearing, it is the grass primarily used in the sod industry. However, Kentucky Bluegrass requires well drained soil and high fertility and moisture levels. It is a sun lover and does not do well in shade: some varieties tend to get mildew in shade. It is slow to germinate when seeded, and slow to become established.

The second most common lawn grasses are the fescues: Creeping Red, Chewings, Hard and Sheep Fescue. Creeping Red Fescue produces rhizomes, or underground shoots, just like Kentucky Bluegrass. It is an excellent grass for dry areas: it grows along many of our main roads in Ontario. It tolerates low rainfall and has a low cultural requirement: it is better underfed than overfed. When it is cut at 2.5 cm height or lower, it will tend to stress in heat and fade out, and it is also susceptible to red thread and leaf spot disease.

Chewings Fescue, a non-creeping fescue, adapts well to poor soils and requires a low to moderate cultural regime. There are a number of new varieties of this grass. It is denser than Creeping Red Fescue and will tolerate closer mowing. It will not tolerate too much fertilizer, heat or wet soils and it also has some susceptibility to leaf spot. Both this grass and Kentucky Bluegrass tend to thatch, which chokes the grass plants. If Chewings Fescue is overwatered and overfed, it gets very thick in the base and more susceptible to disease. Hard Fescue is slower to establish and will tolerate more heat and salt, but it will not tolerate a close cut.

One of the newer grasses for Metro Toronto lawns is Tall Fescue, a grass that adapts well to a wide variety of soils and climates. It can be grown in the cool climates of southern Ontario and in the hotter climates of farther south. The cultural climate necessary for this grass is rather high: Tall Fescue will not tolerate low soil fertility. It can be mowed in heights from 2.5 to 5 cm and is good as a utility grass. Homeowners on busy streets who have salt problems may well be advised to re-sow their boulevards with the Tall Fescue cultivars.

The final species is Perennial Ryegrass. The old coarse ryegrasses were used as nurse crops. Today we have types that are much finer in texture, tolerant of cool weather, and extremely aggressive when used in lawns. Perennial Ryegrass is a bunch type grass and has a low thatch potential. Its plants produce toxins that may have potential for reducing insect populations in the area. Turf-type ryegrasses are tolerant of a soil pH of 6.5 to 8.0, with medium to high fertility. Mowing heights can be as low as 2.5 cm. Perennial Ryegrass is used today for lawn renovation, as it wears well and is adaptable to a wide range of soils. It will tolerate much drier conditions than Kentucky Bluegrass.

Unfortunately Tall Fescue and Perennial Ryegrass are not generally available as sod. The binding ability of Kentucky Bluegrass means it is favoured by sod growers. Subsequently many homeowners end up with Kentucky Bluegrass lawns; even though their soil does not have high fertility and moisture levels. With Toronto's low summer rainfall levels and water restrictions, it makes sense to go with the latter two grasses, which are much more tolerant of adverse conditions.

Tall Fescue   *Kentucky Blue Grass*

CHAPTER 10

PESTS
& DISEASES

While a few small mammals cause damage to plants, the majority of garden pests are insects, including mites, molluscs and eelworms. Additionally, several fungi, bacteria and viruses cause diseases in plants.

TYPES OF DAMAGE

INSECTS AND OTHER TINY ANIMALS

The type of damage caused by insects depends on the feeding habits of the particular insect. Here are the most common kinds:

Sucking • These kinds have needle-like, piercing mouth parts called stylets. They push them into leaves and shoots, to suck out sap. Sometimes at the same time, they inject a digestive enzyme. This results in a small hole and causes irritation. The plant responds with puckered leaves and distorted growth, particularly at the tender shoot tips and in new buds and leaves. Greenfly, blackfly and other plant lice or aphids, leaf hoppers and red spider mites are examples of sucking organisms.

Biting and Chewing • These organisms eat or remove leaves and tender shoots of plants. Signs of their presence are irregular and scallop-shaped leaf margins, totally skeletonized leaves, missing leaves, shoots with pieces taken out of them, and distorted growing tips on new shoots. Biting insects include caterpillars of all kinds, weevils and several beetles.

Rasping • Some insects, and molluscs such as snails and slugs, have rough, sandpaper-like mouth parts. They feed by scraping off the leaf surfaces, leaving obvious open patches and sometimes semi to fully skeletonized areas. As these areas dry out, they may turn brownish and papery. Slugs and pear slugs (sawfly larvae) are examples. Slugs leave silvery trails of mucous.

Mining • Leaf miners lay eggs in between the upper and lower leaf surfaces. The eggs hatch and the larvae tunnel through the leaves, eating the soft inner tissues. Characteristic signs are meandering, whitish lines or irregularly shaped patches. When these patches dry out, they become papery textured and brownish. Birch, lilac and columbine leaf miners are common.

Leaf Rolling, Curling and Sticking • Some organisms roll or pucker leaves or shape them into pockets, using sticky substances or silk-like threads. This is done to form a protective hiding place for larvae and pupae. Elm aphids and many caterpillars are typical leaf rolling organisms.

UNDERSTANDING INSECT LIFE CYCLES

Many insects hatch from eggs laid by mature adults, emerging as larvae (caterpillars, worms and slug-worms etc.). The larvae feed on the leaves, flowers, shoots, buds, and roots of their host plants. When fully developed, the larvae are transformed into pupae or chrysalids which become quiescent, resting for a time. Finally, adults emerge from the pupae to feed, mate and reproduce. While there are many variations in life cycles, this description serves as a general model. Some specific life cycles are discussed below.

Aphids • Aphids or plant lice (also called greenfly and blackfly), scale insects, white-flies, mealy bugs and several other insects do not follow this life cycle. While developing from eggs, they may skip the larvae and pupal stages. Instead, they develop immediately into adult-like forms called nymphs and after going through one or more moults, change into adults.

Larvae, nymphs and adult insects may cause damage to plants.

Mites • Mites are related to the true spiders but don't have clearly defined body segments. They are generally much smaller than spiders. They have six legs when young and eight when adult. Common red spider mites are not easily seen with the naked eye. They can cause extensive damage to plants, through all stages of their life cycle, except when they are in egg form.

Eelworms • Eelworms, or nematodes, are minute, often microscopic, worm-like creatures, tapered at each end. Young and mature forms cause damage by burrowing into and living within various parts of their hosts.

These tiny creatures multiply within the plant tissues, causing distorted growth of leaves, shoots, flowers, bulbs, buds and roots, depending on the characteristics of the eelworm species and host plant. Some cause cysts on roots and others stimulate the growth of galls (roughly round-shaped growths) on shoots. Many kinds are difficult to control.

DISEASES AND VIRUSES

DAMAGE CAUSED

Symptoms of both fungal and bacterial disease include discolouration, thread-like or bumpy growths, rotting, or wilting of any parts of a plant. Specific signs to look for are:

• shoot and root blight: sudden browning or blackening of leaves and young shoots, and curled shoot tips

• layers of whitish or greyish fungal threads on leaves, young shoots and shoot tips

• spots on leaves and fruits

• raised or depressed cankers or lesions on stems

• shoot, fruit or root rot

• wilting of a part of or an entire plant

• galls on the plant stem, at or just above the soil level

Symptoms of virus diseases include distorted or stunted growth, or discolouration in leaf veins. Specifically, watch for:

- distorted growth of leaves, stems and flowers
- various shaped patterns of yellow, pale green and green on the leaves, often resembling tiny mosaics
- stunted growth and smaller-than-normal leaves
- yellowing between the leaf veins, or pale-coloured to transparent veins on leaves
- generally slow or limited growth

LIFE CYCLES

Fungi • Fungus diseases usually begin their life cycles as spores. These have a similar function to that of seeds in flowering plants. Spores sprout or germinate on leaves, shoots and roots etc., producing minute, thread-like growths that either run over the surface of the plant or, later, inside the plant tissues. They go through an often-complicated life cycle, finally producing adult spore bearing bodies which repeat the cycle.

Bacteria • Bacteria infect plants as spores or live cells. They don't develop thread-like growths like fungi, although some kinds produce chains of cells. Usually they are single celled, growing and multiplying within the body of the host plant. They usually gain entry into the plant through wounds or natural openings, as they cannot penetrate a plant's cuticle or skin.

Most fungal and bacterial diseases are parasitic: the invading organisms are dependent on the host for survival.

Viruses • Viruses are submicroscopic organisms that invade plant cells and interfere with normal cell functions. They can only multiply and survive within the plants, which often then die. Viruses are infectious and are often transmitted by sucking insects. They may also be spread through pruning activity or other handling of the plants.

There are no dependable chemical controls for viruses.

CONTROL

Effective control of pests and diseases starts with regular inspection and prevention such as frequent hoeing, watering and attentive care. However, if a problem does come up, it is important to know how to select the appropriate control method.

REGULAR INSPECTION

The first line of defense is regular inspection. The time to take action is when the first few bugs or spots are noticed, before the infestation has reached epidemic proportions. Check every plant in the garden every week. Learn to recognize the early warning symptoms: a half rolled leaf, a growing tip just a bit off centre or slightly twisted, one or two aphids or caterpillars, a dull sheen on leaves, or a few leaves at an unnatural angle. By learning to recognize normal, healthy growth, you will be quick to notice deviations. Good gardeners learn to recognize problems at fifty paces.

IDENTIFY THE PROBLEM

To select the proper control method, one must identify the problem accurately. If you cannot identify your pest or disease, your local nursery may be able to help; however you must give them specific information on symptoms and type of bug or damage.

DECIDE THE CONTROL

It's a bad practice to jump to conclusions about pest control, especially when chemical methods are to be used. However, once you have identified the problem, you can determine the appropriate method of control.

There are two basic approaches to control — non-chemical, including biological and cultural, and chemical — both of which are discussed below.

Non-chemical • Healthy, strong, vigorous plants grown in their proper environment are not as susceptible to pests and diseases as those which are neglected and weak or grown in an unfavourable environment. Even when attacked, well grown plants withstand the onslaught and recover much better. Most of non-chemical control involves preventive measures, such as proper spacing of plants, and regular digging, washing and pruning.

Always remove litter that accumulates in the corners and along the base of fences and hedges of the yard. Hoe regularly to eliminate weeds and stir the soil surface to disturb insect eggs, larvae and adults. Remove boards and flat stones that can provide a refuge for slugs and beetles. Be circumspect about piles of firewood — they can act as homes to many insects. Keep the garden clean at all times.

Don't work among or harvest plants when foliage is wet. Avoid breaking, bruising or otherwise damaging plants when walking or working among them.

Remove broken, discoloured, badly diseased and dead stems, shoots and branches from all plants as noticed. Also remove dead branches and leaves from the soil. Cut back into healthy tissue just above and slightly sloping back from a bud or side shoot that is pointing away from the centre of the plant.

Always remove and destroy plants infected by a disease or virus and those seriously affected by blights and wilts.

Avoid over-watering. Frequent watering keeps the soil surface too moist, making it difficult for oxygen to reach plant roots and also create very high levels of humidity during naturally humid periods. Spray with water when the atmosphere is buoyant and moving, not when the weather is dull, overcast and sultry.

Natural Controls
Regular, reasonably forceful spraying with water will keep many pests at bay. Mites in particular do not like water or high humidity. The spray will knock off many bugs and eggs. It will also keep foliage clean.

Every fall, dig over all vegetable plots and flower beds and borders, exposing the soil to the cleansing effect of winter weather. Fork as deeply as practical between established shrubs and herbaceous perennials, short of seriously disturbing their root systems, leaving the soil as level as possible between plants.

If pests do manage to infiltrate your garden, there are several non-chemical methods that can be used to remove them.

Hand picking • Hand picking is a good way to remove insects. Although some people are a bit squeamish about this method, when insect populations are small it is effective and practical. Pick off the bugs and, if you can't abide the thought of squashing them underfoot, drop them into a jar of kerosene to be carefully disposed of later.

Trapping • Night feeders, including slugs, may be trapped under cool, moist hiding places. Flat stones, boards, citrus fruit and cucumber peel, and the leaves of lettuce and cabbage may be laid on the ground overnight. Lift them during the day and destroy the hiding bugs.

Cockroaches, slugs and some other beetles are attracted to beer. Sink a small can or jar of beer in the ground up to its rim. Bugs attracted by the smell will investigate, fall in and drown.

Soapy Water • Water plus a little mild dishwashing detergent or pure soap will provide a measure of control for many pests, particularly the soft-bodied kinds like aphids, leaf hoppers and some caterpillars. An old remedy is 0.5 kilograms of high grade, non-caustic, soft soap, thoroughly mixed with 45 litres of water. Be careful with plants that have a waxy, bluish skin or cuticle such as carnations, pinks and some conifers. The soap solution may melt the wax and discolour the foliage. If in doubt, first test one stem or leaf.

Insecticidal soaps can also be used. They are very popular with environmentally conscious gardeners.

CHEMICAL

There are many effective pesticides. New kinds are being developed each year. The use of chemicals in the home garden is regulated by the federal and provincial governments through their Agriculture and Environment departments.

These bodies approve the kinds of chemicals suitable for home use, and suggest specific formulations and methods of application.

In general, chemical controls fall into these categories: contact insecticides, stomach poisons, systemic insecticides, fumigants, contact fungicides, systemic fungicides and bactericides.

Contact insecticides kill insects on contact or soon thereafter. An insecticide may directly hit the insect or the insect may pick the chemical up on its feet. Many modern insecticides are of this type. Several commonly used kinds are only persistent for 24 - 48 hours, and then break down to harmless compounds. With serious infestations, repeat spraying may be necessary. Contact insecticides are useful in controlling sucking and biting insects.

Stomach poisons coat the plant's leaves with insecticide which is ingested by the insect when it feeds. These are used to control biting and chewing insects.

Systemic insecticides are absorbed by the plant through its leaves and soft stems, and distributed via the sap stream throughout the plant. The insect absorbs the chemical during feeding, wherever it is on or within the plant, no matter what its method of feeding. Since systemics stay inside the plant for a while, they are effective over a longer period than contact insecticides. They are used to control hard-to-hit pests such as leaf miners, leaf rollers, leaf curling aphids, and other persistent insects.

Fumigants are chemicals used to generate poisonous gases or fumes. These are most commonly used to control pests in greenhouses, where the fumes can be confined, or to combat soil borne pests. Fumigants are seldom used by home gardeners, except as a contracted service.

Contact fungicides kill or check the development of fungus diseases on the outside of the plant.

Systemic fungicides are absorbed by the plant and distributed throughout the sap stream. These kinds kill or check the growth of both external and internal fungus diseases.

Bactericides, as their name implies, control bacteria. Many bacteria are hard to control, and there are not too many types of bactericide available. Copper oxychloride formulations are among the commonest. The old fashioned Bordeaux mixture is still used to control some blights. It is made by mixing one part copper sulphate and one part calcium hydroxide in one hundred parts of clean water. If this mix causes burning on foliage, the copper sulphate can be reduced up to one half the amount.

Application Methods • Bearing in mind that it is better to take action before a pest or disease problem reaches epidemic proportions, spot treatments are a good form of control. Rather than dousing the entire garden or even an entire plant, treat only the affected areas, plants or parts, if the problem can be isolated.

You can not always be certain of the extent of the infestation. Some chemicals are effective only if the whole plant is sprayed. Systemic insecticides need to be sprayed over an entire plant in order to get enough pesticide into its sap stream. In any case, it is best to treat the infested area enough to solve the problem the first time, rather than having to repeat your efforts.

The basic methods of application are spraying, dusting, spreading granules and drenching.

Spraying • For spraying, the pesticide is thoroughly mixed with water and, in some applications, a wetting agent or surfactant. Using a pneumatic or pump action sprayer, this mixture is sprayed on the affected plant. A high pressure sprayer, which produces a misty spray made up of fine droplets, is best.

Make sure all pesticides are tightly capped and clearly labelled. Store them in a cool, shaded place out of the reach of children.

There are several types of insecticides available. Emulsifiable concentrates mix readily with water, staying in suspension. Powders mixed with water require continual agitation while spraying.

Safety • It is best to spray when the temperature is above 22°C but not over 26°C, and when it is not very windy. Avoid spraying in strong, direct sunlight, especially when the temperature is over 26°C.

Always spray downwind of yourself, and wear a long-sleeved shirt and long pants. It is important not to allow spray to drift onto neighbours' plants.

Before spraying, read the label, and then follow the manufacturer's directions exactly. The basic spraying technique is to completely cover both sides of the leaves and all stems. Start at the base of the plant with the spray nozzle directed up and work upward, finishing at the top.

Shoot a half container of clean water through the sprayer after spraying to flush out the spray head, pipes and tubes, and rinse out the sprayer a couple of times. Hang it upside down to drain. If it is made of metal, this will also prevent it rusting.

After spraying, be sure to take a shower, or at least wash all exposed skin.

Dusting • For this method, pesticides are mixed with fine particle carriers and dusted onto the plants. It's not easy to get dusts on the undersides of leaves. On the other hand, they are easy to apply to the soil.

Dusts are best applied during still, humid weather. Try to create clouds of dust that drift among the leaves. An old method is to put the powder in a nylon stocking and gently tap it with a piece of wood.

Bellows operated dusting machines are also available.

Distributing Granules • Several pesticides for the control of soil pests are available in granular form. These are broadcast over the soil surface, applied in the bottom of or alongside a seed drill, or worked into the soil.

Drenches • Drenches are liquid formulations applied directly to the soil. They may be systemic pesticides absorbed through plant roots rather than leaves, or non-systemic, aimed at a soil borne pest or disease.

Ontario Government Publications (OMAF) useful to the Home Gardener

TREE FRUITS

Apple and Pear Varieties for the Home Garden 81-006

Fruit Trees in the Home Garden 81-046

Repair Grafting 73-072

Rules for Pruning Fruit Trees 77-006

Cedar Apple Rust and Quince Rust 83-020

Apple Scab 86-028

Blister Spot of Apples

Apple Maggot

Fire Blight of Apple and Pear 78-058

Bitter-Pit Control in Apples 83-008

Oriental Fruit Moth 83-073

Oblique-banded Leaf Roller 83-074

Peach Tree Borers 83-072

Insect and Mite Pests of Peach in Ontario 88-119

Peach Canker 86-034

Peach Leaf Curl 83-071

SMALL FRUITS

Insects and Diseases of Cane Fruits 81-001

Grapes in Home Gardens 85-121

Strawberries for Home Gardens 80-054

Elderberries 77-004

Insect Pests of Grape in Ontario 87-013

VEGETABLES

Home Storage of Vegetables 80-019

Chinese Cabbage Production in Southern Ontario 86-090

Growing Rhubarb 79-019

Growing Asparagus in the Home Garden 87-001

Insect Pests of Asparagus 82-061

Diseases of Asparagus 82-045

Late Blight of Potatoes 79-043

Garlic Production 89-096

Rutabagas (Table Turnips) 87-032

ORNAMENTALS

Herb Gardening 76-016

Fertilizing Trees and Shrubs...Landscape 83-040

Rock Gardens 85-113

Grubs in Lawns 84-049

Controlling Native Creeping Bentgrass 79-094

Low Maintenance Landscape Plants 86-061

Growing and Using Gourds 74-017

Selecting Trees for Landscape Plantings 86-038

Juniper Diebacks 83-085

Planting Trees in the Landscape 89-115

FLOWERS

Garden Irises 85-040

Flowering Annuals for the Home Garden 89-116

MISCELLANEOUS: FERTILIZERS, INSECTS

Peanuts for the Home Garden 86-067

Composting in the Home Garden 79-016

Manure Characteristics 85-109

Hairy Chinch Bugs in Lawns

OMAF PUBLICATION BOOKLETS

Rhododendrons and Azaleas 45

1990-91 Insect and Disease Control in the Home Garden 64

Herbaceous Perennials 358

Training and Pruning Fruit Trees 392

Pruning Ornamentals 483

Free Publications from Agriculture Canada

Gypsy Moth 1516

Container Gardening 1653

Major Pests of Birch and Maple Trees 1718-B

Strawberry Cultivars for Eastern Canada 1744

Pruning Fruit Trees in Your Home Garden (Factsheet) 1773-E

INDEX

Pat Tucker emigrated to Canada in April, 1959 and spent two years greenskeeping at the Sunningdale Golf Course in London, Ontario. After graduating from the Ontario Agricultural College with a degree in horticulture in 1965, he became Head of Grounds at the University of Guelph. He took early retirement in July, 1988 and formed a consulting business, Pat Tucker Associates, specializing in grounds management and in service training programs. Since 1968 he has been involved in course marking and development for Independent Study's Ontario Diploma in Horticulture. Pat is currently a sessional lecturer in the Department of Horticultural Science, University of Guelph. He is past president of the Ontario Shade Tree Council and the Ontario Rock Garden Society. In his spare time he grows rock garden plants, hardy alpines and perennials.

OTHER LONE PINE BOOKS FOR ONTARIO INCLUDE:

Attracting Birds — Elaine Butler

A concise guide to the techniques for attracting birds to your backyard. The perfect book to ensure full enjoyment of your garden and yard. Illustrated.

ISBN 0-919433-87-1 64pp 5 1/2 x 8 1/2 $6.95

Birds of Toronto — Gerald McKeating

A beautifully illustrated, full-colour guide to the commonly found birds of Toronto. Excellent for the beginning and intermediate birder.
Colour illustrations.

ISBN 0-919433-63-4 144pp 5 1/2 x 8 1/2 $9.95

Birds of Ottawa — Gerald McKeating

For residents and visitors in the Ottawa region, a beautifully illustrated, full-colour guide to the commonly found birds of the area. Excellent for the beginning and intermediate birder. Colour illustrations.

ISBN 0-919433-64-2 144pp 5 1/2 x 8 1/2 $9.95

The Bicycle Guide to Southwestern Ontario — Gary Horner

The essential book for experienced and novice cyclists alike. Includes detailed directions and background on more than thirty tours. Also advice on bicycle selection, safety tips, equipment and clothing purchase. Illustrated, maps.

ISBN 0-919433-58-8 224pp 5 1/2 x 8 1/2 $9.95

The Lone Pine Picnic Guide to Ontario — Nancy Gibson & John Whittaker

A unique and entertaining guide to over 40 picnic spots throughout the province with information on local history, picnic menus, and things to see and do for each location. Hundreds of appetizing recipes are included. Illustrated, maps.

ISBN 0-919433-69-3 272pp 5 1/2 x 8 1/2 $11.95

Ski Ontario — Gary Horner (available Fall, 1991)

A must-have for the avid skier. Includes descriptions of ski areas throughout the province and sections on choosing ski equipment and clothing. Illustrated, maps.

ISBN 0-919433-93-6 256pp 5 1/2 x 8 1/2 $14.95

Buy these and other Lone Pine books from your local bookstore or order directly from Lone Pine Publishing, #206, 10426 - 81 Avenue, Edmonton, Alberta, T6E 1X5.
Phone: (403) 433 9333 Fax: (403) 433 9646